DON'T
Tell Me What to Do!

DON'T
Tell Me What to Do!

A
Catholic
Understanding of
Modern Moral
Issues

by Father Dave Heney

Paulist Press
New York/Mahwah, N.J.

Cover & interior design by Lynn Else

Library of Congress Cataloging-in-Publication Data

Heney, Dave, 1952-
    Don't tell me what to do! : a Catholic understanding of modern moral issues / by Dave Heney.
      p. cm.
    Includes bibliographical references.
    ISBN 0-8091-4074-8 (alk. paper)
    1. Christian ethics—Catholic authors. I. Title: Don't tell me what to do. II. Title.

BJ1249 .H52 2002
241'.042—dc21

                                2002019165

Published by Paulist Press
997 Macarthur Boulevard
Mahwah, New Jersey 07430

www.paulistpress.com

Printed and bound in the United States of America

Table of Contents

In gratitude

This book developed from a series of adult education programs conducted in several parishes in southern California. I would like to thank those who helped in all stages of its writing. I especially remember the "Catch the Spirit" team from Holy Angels Church in Arcadia, California, the "Semester at St. Monica's" team in Santa Monica, California, the "Waters in the Desert" team at St. Maximilian Kolbe in Westlake Village, California, my Jesus Caritas prayer group, as well as Joyce and David Bock, Les and Marnie LoBaugh, Kathleen E. McCann, Michael and Denise Harvey, Betty Ply, Delis Alejandro, Patricia Conaty, Msgr. Jeremiah McCarthy, Michael and Patricia Horan, Msgr. Peter O'Reilly, and of course, my family, in which I first learned how to live well.

CHAPTER 1

Too Many Moral Voices

Do you want more moral rules in your world, or do you feel you have enough? Do you wonder where you can find help and not be confused by what you hear? Who can you trust when there are so many voices speaking about moral issues today? Does religion really have anything positive to offer? How about the media? Or science? How can we tell if one voice is better than another?

Certainly, some moral voices seem louder than others or use more persuasive tools like television or advertising to advocate the way to live. Other voices can be just as firm and insistent, only quieter. Yet all seem to speak at once in a confusing jangle of demands and of course, always predict some pain or sadness if not followed. This shouting about moral issues can inflame relationships and make honest, thoughtful, dialogue difficult. Maybe you have already met intolerant or arrogant people who lecture in condescending ways and give blunt directions about how we are to live. Maybe you feel like shouting, *"Don't tell me what to do!"* No wonder people are confused, and even angry, about morality today. How can we discover what is good behavior? Where can we find wisdom? To whom can we go to find answers *and* respect for ourselves as persons? Where are the answers we can trust?

Some say morality was clearer in the past. That may be true, but, rather than looking back to the 1950s, 1940s, or even earlier decades for guidance, perhaps we can go farther back for help. Maybe we should return to the very beginning of everything, to the very earliest story of human behavior. We will begin our search all the way back, past the writings of theologians, the words of St. Paul in the Epistles, and even the words of Our Lord in the Gospels, and return to the earliest biblical story of moral relationships: the dramatic and compelling story of Adam and Eve.

With Adam and Eve in Paradise

Catholics base much of our moral understanding of human relationships on the two biblical stories of the creation, nature, and purpose of Adam and Eve. You will find them where right they belong: in Genesis, the very first book of the bible. The first story in Genesis 1:26–31 reveals our *simultaneous* creation as men and women for the purpose of *controlling* the Earth, whereas the second in Genesis 2:4–25 reveals a *sequential* creation for the purpose of *helping* each other and *caring* for the environment. The Genesis author was inspired by God to include both stories and so provide a more complete telling of who we are and what we are to do. God placed powerful but subtle ideas about behavior in these accounts. We will look at them closely, for they reveal the road to true and lasting happiness.

Taken together, these two stories say a lot about love, commitment, and the right way to treat each other. They tell us about God as well. God is the completely free, autonomous, and completely *giving* being. No one told God to create the world and then give it to us. It was all a free gift. God created these first two people in that very same image, to be free and giving. The central idea about who we are comes from a simple but majestic phrase in Genesis: *Imago Dei*. It is Latin for "in the image of God." What is that image? God created our first ancestors and gave them *freedom* (Gen 2:16), *equality* (Gen 1:27; 2:23), and *goodness* (Gen 1:31). He created them to be *for each other as giving helpmates* (Gen 2:18) and to *worship* Him (Gen 4:3). These words share similar ideas for they define subtle shades of the same human dignity and so reveal our answer. A moral life always affirms these virtues and keeps them in harmony and *balance*. Let's take a closer look at each of these similar "Garden virtues." On these we will base much of what Catholics understand about morality.

Equality ■ We are equal to each other before God in dignity and honor and therefore deserving of the utmost regard and respect from every person. Of course, we vary a great deal in psychological and physiological talents and abilities, but we have the same value and dignity as human beings. Precisely because we are from the Lord means we are each—men and women—equal in worth and equal in human dignity. We deserve to be treated with honor and respect. (Put simply, any friend of God must be a friend of mine!) Therefore, no one can claim ownership of another adult or control his or her behavior. In Genesis, Adam is not the "boss" of Eve, nor is Eve the "boss" of Adam. Neither may control nor possess the other as an object or thing. We are never *possessions* of each other, but *expressions* of God, who considers us individual treasures of great value. From this equality we learn we cannot command or give orders to other adults about what to do, what to think or feel, or how to be, as if we were superior beings. We are not ultimately in charge of life or its moral code. That means no person, on *his or her own authority*, can tell another adult person how to live life. The cry of "Don't tell me what to do" rings true.

Of course, parents and teachers may guide children in their care, and government agencies, employers, and even neighborhoods may also exercise appropriate control over our lives but only with our willing cooperation as citizens in a democracy or as employees in a job we have freely chosen. We voluntarily cede control over certain aspects of our lives for the greater good of our family, our education, the larger community, or our job. We agree to stop at red lights, wear appropriate business dress to work, and obey thousands of civic laws set by others so that all kinds of different people can live together in a peaceful society. It is control by consent. We still remain equal before God.

Freedom ■ God gave us the power to choose (Gen 2:16) and that has made all the difference. This personal autonomy reveals we are not simply preprogrammed robots automatically fulfilling some prearranged plan. Our future is not predestined or set in concrete. We can *consciously choose* our way and make decisions about this or that behavior according to our own way of thinking. In a profound way, this freedom makes us human. We can choose our own path of behavior. Trees cannot. Rocks cannot. A tree cannot choose to absorb too little water, nor can a rock choose to lie still. We can. God gave us free will and that freedom is fundamental to our humanity. Even though people often settle quickly into predictable routines of habit and custom, we are still free to change. We have the freedom to help ourselves and improve our life or *even go against our own nature* and do something harmful to ourselves. That's how powerful freedom is, and God will not interfere with it.

We can choose to love or choose to hate. We can choose, know that we are choosing, and choose pretty much whatever we want. Yet every choice will have consequences. Those choices may provide us with moments of pride and accomplishment or times of sorrow and pain. We can determine so much of the quality of our existence—all from this power of choosing. Additionally, our choices reveal our personal stance in the world, our way of seeing things, our ideas, feelings, and behaviors. In short, our choices reveal our personality. To a large extent, we are our choices.

Goodness ■ God created us as good persons but not in the way we usually think of goodness. We are good simply because God created us and not for any good or bad behaviors on our part. God does not love us because *we* are good. We are good because *He* loves us. That's a big difference. His love is a unilateral action on His part alone, not connected to our good or bad behavior. God loves us no matter what we do. In a sense, it is too late to lose or change His love by our bad behavior. He already likes us—irrevocably, permanently, and deeply—and there is nothing we can do about it (Rom 8:39). That makes a lot of sense, really, when you reflect on it. His affection could not be in response to our perfect behavior. After all, our life is certainly a mixed bag of good and bad behavior, and it will always be that way. No one acts well or badly all the time, yet it is precisely God's love that makes us "good," not our actions.

Most likely, we will never be perfect or sinless in our life, but we can, at least, be honest about it. Our Lord does not expect perfection—just honesty. After all, how can we be perfect without His grace? We make many mistakes, errors of judgment, and bad decisions constantly. We must call them for what they are: mistakes, errors, and bad choices. That is simple honesty. The truth about our life, the good and bad events, is what the Lord wants to hear from us. Yet our fundamental goodness as persons comes not from our efforts, whether successes or failures, but arises from the interest, attention, and love God has for us. That interest from God initiates the next step in faith—our response. If we respond by loving as He does, well, we simply call that moral living.

Service to others ■ God made no mistakes in our creation. He did not create Adam incomplete or inadequate, until there was Eve. However, it was not "good" for the "one" to be alone. It did not make sense for there to be only one person because our purpose is to love. The sequential creation of Eve in the second creation account simply affirms that our *purpose* in life is to be in relationships, to be in caring, giving, for-the-other relationships. We were made for love.

Although each person is created complete and whole, our purpose or finality is not realized until we share our life with others. For example, a newly made car is "complete" when finished on the assembly line, but it only really fulfills its purpose when it is actually driven. Even then, it operates best when operated according to its manufacturer's instructions. In the same way, Adam is complete when created but only fulfills his purpose by being in a loving and intimate relationship with another person, just as his "manufacturer" designed him to love. There must be someone else around to love, so God had to create more people. God designed all of us to want that kind of intimate sharing and self-revelation with another. Adam needed an Eve, and Eve needed an Adam. We were made to *want* to be with another. We were designed to help and serve our fellow Earth-dwellers, to take care of and watch out for them, and in a thousand different ways, to give of ourselves to others. It is just our nature.

Worship ■ We did not make the world or ourselves or set things up the way they are. We simply "discovered it all" in our occasional spontaneous moments of awareness throughout our life. In a sense, we "found" ourselves alive and here in this place. With that discovery, each living moment reveals a sense that there is a God of the universe and that all of life is a gift. Gratitude is our fundamental experience of faith. Gratitude is our response to the discovery of our life and its origin in God.

We acknowledge God's place in the universe and in our life with worship. It is the behavior and ritual of gratitude. In reverential acts of worship, we simply acknowledge with rites and ceremonies that someone else is in charge and that we are not in total control of the way things are. Worship, then, is always an act of gratitude. Worship reveals God as, well, the most Supreme Being. Worship reminds us to look to God first for true wisdom.

Balance ■ Life was in balance and harmony in the Garden. Adam and Eve gave love to each other, and they both gave love back to the Lord in worship. They knew they did not bring themselves or the world into existence, so they chose to see everything—the world and each other—as a gift. They were stewards of creation, not its masters. *What they received as gifts, they gave as gifts, to God and to each other.* They helped each other enjoy life to the fullest, and they helped each other enjoy God. Neither usurped the role of the other. They did not try to be God, and God let them be humans by respecting their human freedom.

Everything was in the right balance and perspective. Everything operated according to the "manufacturers instructions." That balance describes the "right way" of doing things and is the basis for understanding moral behavior. Perspective, or balance, is the beginning of wisdom. Everything changed, as it changes for us today, when that balance was upset. Adam and Eve got things out of place.

The First Sin Is the Only Sin

The first sin was to "damage" our humanity. We damaged our human nature to love well. In that dramatic encounter in Genesis, the serpent tempted Adam and Eve to lose something of those God-given qualities that made them human. The fruit they ate was from the "Tree of Knowledge of Good and Evil." To the Jews, only God knew all that was good and evil, so the fruit was actually a symbol of the knowledge and total power of God. The serpent tempted them to take that supreme power in to their lives, *to be all-powerful gods themselves,* unneedful and unhelpful to each other. They ate, or "ingested," the fruit of the Tree of Godlike Power. Satan's temptation must have sounded attractive. Being a god meant they would not need each other and could even control the freedom of the other person. Power is attractive at first, but ironically, it makes us weak. Satan tempted them to be unfree and *captive slaves to their own whims and desires.* No freedom there. Not caring for the other, they thought only of themselves and even blamed each other for the whole event! They upset the balance of nature—their manufacturer's instructions.

That first sin is in a real sense the only sin. All the sins we commit today are types of that first desire for excessive self-sufficiency. Every sin creates an imbalance in the true relationship we have with each other and God. Adam and Eve got what they asked for in a way. Human relationships from that moment forward took on the character of seeking power over others and self-centeredness (Gen 3:16). They took on the

9

potential to be manipulative and controlling. Sin makes us a little inhuman. Even God has to ask when he is looking for Adam, "Where are you?" (Gen 3:9). It is as if He is asking, "Where is the one I created? You have made yourself into someone else!" Sin changes us into something other than what God created. It goes against our own nature and our own best interests, and it results in a world we would rather not have were we thinking clearly. It shoots us in our own foot.

Sin is contagious too. Precisely because we are so inclined to relationships means we can affect each other profoundly for good or evil. The very next story in the Bible is the story of Cain and Abel—a story of revenge, jealousy, and violence. Sin can pass from person to person, from Adam to Cain, from me to you. That now pervasive condition of human life, that easy inclination to sin, that legacy of Adam and Eve is called, "Original Sin." We are not personally guilty of this Original Sin, for it is not a personal choice. We are just deeply affected by it, for we live in a world where it is so easy to sin, to hurt and be hurt.

The Way Back to the Garden

All of the scriptures, all of the Bible stories, much of our faith really, is about getting back to the Garden and to God, or returning to our real human nature. That is the "salvation" about which we hear so much. In the Garden, we can be our full human selves and find God. Only then will we be happy and at peace. All the stories of Abraham, Moses, and the Prophets are God's way of teaching, showing, and guiding us back to Garden relationships. Finally, God sent His Son. *"I have come that you might have life and have it to the fullest!"* (John 10:10). *"I have come that my joy may be yours and your joy may be complete"* (John 15:11). *He is the Way, the Truth, and the Life* (John 14:6). St. Augustine, a profound Christian philosopher and bishop in the fourth century, summarized it well in a deeply felt prayer to God: "Our hearts are restless until they rest in you."

This is not nostalgia for some forgotten tropical paradise. It is a return to who we actually are. It is a "coming back to our real self." For example, some people, after many years, will return to their hometown and reconnect with the experiences and values that started their life's journey. They might discover how much the pressures of life had changed them over the years, perhaps in ways they don't like. Perhaps they rekindle forgotten values or even friendships. There is a sense of the hometown person as "real" and the "later" person as a "detour." They feel happy to be "themselves" again.

The point of Jesus' whole time on Earth was our complete, total, and full happiness with God and each other, even in the midst of our living in this difficult world. We can return "home" and find joy no matter where we live. Everything God made He made precisely for us to be happy. The whole point of our even knowing the Lord, of knowing our faith, of experiencing Jesus is to receive the gift of joy, the fullness of life, and the profound peace that only He can give. He will show us the way to treat each other that will bring these gifts. They can be ours, even in the midst of this world filled with people who still continue to choose badly! Jesus came not so much to change the world, but to change us. We can spend our time in no better way than to discover that "way" of the Lord. Let us hope we each freely choose it.

Free Will: Our Power of Choice

Do we actually have free will? What happens in our actual experience of choosing? Do we really have the power to make choices? Our free will develops from three unique abilities that are part of our natural makeup as rational human beings. Together these three abilities contribute to what is needed to make a moral choice.

First, we are able to see the *consequences* of our actions. That means we can literally imagine the future. I can anticipate that if I do this certain action, then that result will follow. For example, if I throw a rock at a window, I know it will break, and I can kind of already "see" it happen in my mind. Second, we are able to make *value judgments* about which choice is better than the other. We can put all the options in some kind of order and rate them according to some criteria that make sense, even if only to ourselves. For example, I can list several targets for my rock, starting with the biggest window first. Third, we can actually *make a final choice*. We are able to let go of all options in favor of just one. If we choose one target window to break, then all the others remain intact. That may seem obvious, but the idea of letting go of something is actually fairly sophisticated. We come to understand that we cannot go down two roads at once and that choosing one path means we will never know what the other was like at this particular moment in time. These dynamics are the foundation for making choices.

Some people question if we really have freedom of choice. They believe we are predetermined by our genes, or social environment, or other cultural factors to act in certain ways. If so, then we cannot be held responsible for what was, after all, not our choice. For example, it may be that certain genes predispose some people to alcoholism. Well, certainly many biological and social factors influence our decisions, but nothing can change the brute fact of our personal *experience* of freedom. In our hearts, we simply feel free. We sense our acts are voluntary and under our control, and so they remain our personal responsibility. Even if everything I do is actually preordained somewhere, it doesn't really help me in my moment of choosing because I cannot know what that pre-ordained decision is. I still feel free to decide. Of course, other factors can limit and diminish my responsibility for specific actions. For example, lack of education, ignorance, mental illness, stress, longtime habit, and severe trauma can limit my freedom and so diminish responsibility in specific instances.

This power of choice is part of our natural makeup as human beings. It doesn't have to be taught, in a sense, because it develops naturally in our personality and actually may be one of the reasons for our evolutionary success. However, while our ability to predict consequences and make judgments grows naturally from our human genetic programming, the specific set of moral criteria we might use to make these judgments does not. These criteria arise out of culture, religion, and family relationships and are passed down to us

almost from the first moments of infancy. Sometimes parents
or teachers teach them directly, and sometimes we just assim-
ilate them naturally from our social and cultural environment.
We may be consciously aware of them or not, but they form
the rules for choosing this or that action. It is these moral
guidelines that tell us whether to throw the rock, to not
throw it at all, or to change from the impulse of throwing
rocks into the more rewarding skill of throwing baseballs.

There are many sets of moral systems in the world
today, from the large religions to the small cults and even to
individual people. In fact, it is a rather common opinion in
some circles today that each person must set up his or her
very own personal moral code. How can we know what is a
good system? What is the best set of moral guides that will
make our lives happier, more fulfilled, and more joyful?

Pope John Paul II responded in a 1993 letter to the
world called "The Splendor of Truth." He asks the question,
"Who knows what is good?" He begins with a story from
Matthew 19:16. A rich young man approaches Jesus and asks,
"What good must I do to achieve eternal Life?" That is such
an important question. It is ours as well when we ponder
morality (and mortality), for we wonder so often about the
right course of action for our family and ourselves. What is
the good thing to do? Jesus answers the young man by list-
ing the Ten Commandments and the additional invitation to
"follow" Him with his whole heart and soul. The question
coupled with the response from Jesus link salvation with
behavior. He reveals there is a "way of living" that is better
than others, and it is built into our nature.

14

Most important to the passage is that the man asked *Jesus* for the answer. He knew that only God is the real source of knowing what is good and evil and somehow felt Jesus could speak God's voice. Remember how we discussed the story of Genesis and the name of one of the trees in the Garden of Eden. According to this interpretation, the Tree of Knowledge of Good and Evil was reserved for God alone. That reservation preserves and safeguards our equality with each other, for it is not for any person to tell anyone else what is good or evil based on one's self alone. My idea of the good cannot take precedence over yours. It is up to all of us to discern what *God* has revealed. Yet *His* idea of goodness does take precedence over ours! We need to know that will of God and know it genuinely.

We believe Jesus gave the job of discerning and authentically proclaiming His will to the church (Matt 16:19). While it is certainly not the only place God reveals Himself, it is one place Jesus declared God could be found for sure (Matt 18:20). We believe the church possesses the fullest revelation of what God wants to say to us. Can we actually say that about a community with people in it like you and me? God is present there not because of the holiness or weakness of its members, but because He wants to be there. That behavior makes more sense, really. God has principally chosen to reveal Himself in a family, and families are never perfect. Neither are the people in the church. The God of the universe, who is love itself, makes His own nature visible, not only in individuals, but also where both strong and weak people struggle in relationships, such as in His church.

Remember: God did not stop creating people when Adam and Eve made their mistake but continued with the rest of us as well. He gives us the same freedom they had to love or hate. Together, precisely in our struggle to choose wisely, we reveal the presence and goodness of God.

Because this goodness is built into our nature, it follows that it cannot fundamentally change, but anything that hinders our freedom, equality, or service will always be harmful. However, if we sincerely choose something evil—not realizing that it is so—our personal responsibility is lessened. Still, we can never call that action good, even if done for good intentions. There just isn't a good excuse for going against the way we were made.

The Commandments list some of those evils as a kind of lower limit of behavior below which we cannot go. The Commandments have both positive (thou shalt honor…) and negative sections (thou shalt not…), but the negatives are only the lower limits of behavior. For example, while it is true that we may not be able to honor our parents or praise God perfectly, and we may not love others very well, at least we don't kill them, use them as objects, or steal from them. "Thou shalt not…" is the minimum standard.

Even though we might fail for a variety of reasons and our personal culpability might be lessened for sincere mistakes, those wrong actions can never be called "good." Beautiful intentions may lessen responsibility but cannot change an evil act into a good one. The end cannot justify the means. While this sounds like an impossible standard, it is not our perfection that makes us moral. It is our integrity. We may never be perfect, but we can, at the very least, be honest about our behavior.

The moment we honestly admit the mistake, we might also feel something else: a sense of guilt. What happens next is very important because guilt can either be wonderfully healing or disastrously destructive. It is that powerful. Some people today may still nurse wounds received long ago from harsh critics of their behavior. Reactions can vary a lot from that legacy of trauma. While some might now reject *anyone* setting common moral rules or standards, others remain too afraid to move for fear of even the littlest criticism. Both are tragic results. Misunderstanding guilt takes us far from the joy God wants us to have. Misunderstanding the goodness of our own conscience takes us far from the trust God places within us. We are going to make mistakes; there is no doubt about that. So learning about guilt and conscience is essential to having a good moral attitude—one that is healthy and mature.

Conscience and guilt need not battle each other, but we will look at these powerful events in more detail.

Discussion Starters

These questions are meant to jump-start conversation in a discussion group or continue some further reflection for yourself about this chapter.

1. How do you feel when a friend tells you what to do about something in your private life? What about a teacher? A clergyman? A stranger?

2. How would you advise a good friend about an important moral issue?

3. What is your image of God today? How has it changed at significant times in your life?

4. God allowed Adam and Eve to suffer the natural consequences of their sin. If you were God, would you have done anything different?

5. Describe a time when you felt especially "good." What were the things about that event that helped you feel this way?

6. What were your thoughts when you read in this chapter that God made us free and equal?

CHAPTER 2

Feeling Guilty

"What should I do in this situation? What is the right thing to do?" ("And what will I actually end up doing?") These are the sorts of questions we should ask ourselves before we act, when we are trying to choose behavior. Afterward we might ask, "Should I have done that? Was that choice OK?" However, we also make *judgments* about those acts as well. "That was a terrible thing to do! I feel awful about what happened! I never should have done that!" It is part of the inner conversation that goes on in our head. We can understand these two powerful interior events as *voices* that we hear in our mind. Before we act, we hear the voice of conscience. After we act, we might also hear the voice of guilt.

Guilt can be either healthy or unhealthy in our relationships. Healthy guilt helps distinguish when I am not being true to myself *as God made me,* and it helps me to see the true proportion in the relationship of when I might be selfish. Healthy guilt is a good conscience that is positive, self-confident, *and always encouraging.* Healthy guilt says we can change for the better. Unhealthy guilt sees my entire life as bad or not true to someone else's expectations of myself. It is usually a kind of "voice" we hear from habit that says change is impossible. Unhealthy guilt helps no one and is actually another form of imbalance. It is important to distinguish these two kinds of guilt.

Listening to Our Conscience

How do we know what to do? Well, we look at the facts, consult some moral standard, and make a choice. However, we believe that there are certain choices that are naturally part of our makeup and lead to good mental and spiritual health. We believe that God designed us to want happiness, success, and fulfillment. We believe He *wants* those gifts for us also. In fact, He designed us to seek the behaviors that provide them. God made certain behaviors more effective in providing happiness and joy. If we do them, we will be happy. Just like our car, we operate best when we operate according to our manufacturer's instructions. Because these are "hard-wired" behaviors in our genetic code as human beings, we call them part of the Natural Law. They are the way things are. Good behaviors are those that fulfill, encourage, or foster the four main "Garden of Eden virtues" of *freedom, equality, goodness,* and *service to one another.* Wrong behaviors are those that prevent, deter, or diminish those virtues in any way. They help no one.

Freedom respects the autonomy and dignity of each person. God respects our freedom and ability to know and do good. He does not interfere. *Equality* affirms that God is above us, and only He knows what is really good. We cannot tell each other what to do on our own authority. *Goodness* verifies that our dignity and worth come from God's interest in ourselves at the moment of our conception and not in our own behavior later. If God loves us that much, then we must love ourselves as well. Finally, *service* affirms that real happiness comes from a life that is spent in giving to others. When that giving is mature, there is no sense of loss or emptiness. A giving person feels even more complete for having served others.

A good conscience is the voice in our head that tells us to do those loving behaviors. However, it doesn't tell us exactly what they are in everyday life. Our intellect must tell us that. That's why we must study, think, ponder, and reflect on our experience and learn from others who have gone before us to really understand this natural law in the world today. That's why we look to authentic church teachers, to whom Jesus told us to look. Although the truth is almost instinctive, we can easily miss it, for we are often tempted to choose other ways we think will make us happy. But they work only for a short time of immediate gratification and ultimately do not satisfy. Our freedom ironically allows us to choose behaviors against our own best interests. For example, people choose to take drugs, drink too much, or think badly of themselves. These behaviors may work for a short time, but the behaviors God designed for our good are the only ones that lead to lasting happiness. Once we know the God-given good behavior, conscience is that voice that tells us to do it.

Even though this natural law is universal to all human beings throughout history, we can easily miss it. Because one of our greatest skills is denial, and because no person can claim to know the good on their own, *God has made good behavior known to us in ways we can understand. That message He gave to humanity in our nature, and especially through the people He specifically called to live this behavior, first the "chosen people" and now the church, through Jesus Christ.* Jesus said, "I will be with you always even to the end of the world" (Matt 28:20). We call that message "Revelation." Part of revelation was written much later in what are now called the scriptures or the Bible. The revelation of God guides our life always. Only He knows the good actions to do. Only His voice do we follow. We can look to the actual behavior of Jesus, Our Savior and Lord, as a model. If we want to know how to live, look to the Lord and especially at how He handled conscience and guilt.

Listening to the Voice of Jesus

The crowds that heard Jesus were volatile. One day, the crowd was overjoyed at the Lord's message and wanted to make Him a king (Mark 1:37). The next day they tried to stone Him (Mark 6:1). One could go crazy being a Messiah! However, Jesus always remained true to Himself. He never changed the message, or compromised, or backtracked from the set agenda. That message was set by His Father in Heaven. *"Don't you know I must be about my Father's business?"* (Luke 2:49). He was always true to His Father's will. That's precisely how He was able to remain consistent, authentic, and genuine throughout His life. He did not have to be a different person in every situation. He was always authentic.

Knowing the good, His conscience urged Him to do that behavior and *only* that good behavior.

Conscience is in a real sense the voice of God in our hearts telling us to do the good behaviors that He has *already* set in our nature for our real happiness. It is the exact same voice that Jesus heard. It will also keep us steady in volatile situations, just as for the Lord. Because the voice comes from God, the church cannot change it in any way and certainly not because of the wishes of the crowd. Opinion polls are not where we look for that voice. We cannot look to personal whims or passing fads for truth. We need something more solid. We look where He told us to look. "I *am* the Way, the Truth, and the Life" (John 14:6). When we follow that voice there is no regret, no looking back, no second thoughts. We can finally sleep the sleep of a good conscience!

Healthy and Unhealthy Voices

After some action or choice, the voice we hear might be guilt. Guilt is the voice that says we might have chosen badly and against the voice that said to act differently. Guilt is the voice that battles conscience. This experience of inner battle can either be healthy or unhealthy. It's either a burden or wonderful opportunity. Unhealthy guilt is like a voice that hounds us and shouts down any goodness we might feel. It colors our entire life with an awful blackness. It can make us miserable and is a great tragedy for some in the church. It is extremely important to understand the voices of good and bad guilt. The message we hear about our behavior is important. However, was that message or opinion correct? Was that voice the voice of God? Should we really have followed it? If not God, whose voice was it? How can we tell the difference?

We know there are all kinds of voices around telling us what to do. Family, friends, neighbors, fellow workers, our boss at work—it seems everyone has an opinion of what we should do. But they are external voices to us. They are from other people who don't have our history. We also, in a sense, "hear" a voice from within ourselves as well. That inner voice can come from two sources. It may be a "ghost" voice from our past, or it may be from God.

A "ghost" voice is a way of describing the voice of an actual person in our life who was extremely important to us but is no longer around. Perhaps he or she died or moved away. It might have been a parent, or teacher, or some significant person whose opinion we felt to be very powerful and important. This person probably spoke often about our behavior and the things we did. To this day perhaps we can still "hear" him or her. If this person were especially important to us as children, then we tend to retain those messages for a while even after that person is gone. That's a good thing. That's how we develop as people, learn things, and mature. However, as a child, we would not have had the maturity or wisdom to put a good or bad voice in perspective. After all, it takes some maturity to distinguish the helpful one from the harmful one. How can we determine today that this voice we hear is the one God wants us to hear? How do we know this voice is for our benefit and will help us grow? The behavior of Jesus in the scriptures tells us everything we need to know about the voice of Our Father in Heaven.

God's voice is always and only *encouraging*. We understand God's voice through the words and deeds of Jesus, and He always used sinful behavior as an *opportunity* for the sinner to change, mature, repent, and grow in holiness. The sin was never the end of the story but a door to a new and happier life. Jesus was more interested in the *recovery* of the sinner than in the sin itself (Luke 15:7; Matt 18:13). Of course, He always acknowledged the sin and acknowledged the damage it caused, but He always invited the sinner in love to put it behind and learn from it (John 8:11). His words were always "encouraging" in the true sense of that word: to give courage. Our Lord believes in us. He affirms that with His grace we *can* change, repent, and grow. After all, that we will sin at some point is almost guaranteed. That we sin is no surprise to Jesus. That we can recover and return to holiness is the real story. *How we recover says more about our character than the sins we commit.* A voice that acknowledges the sin but invites growth and change is a good and healthy guilt. Listen to the voice of the Lord in the following scripture passages. They each involve a person who committed some serious sin, and in each, Jesus invites a change for the better. Mark 10:21: the story of the rich young man. John 8:11: the woman caught in adultery. Luke 5:8: Peter's sinfulness. Luke 7:37: the penitent woman.

Any other voice that says anything different from encouragement is suspect. For example, some religion teachers might use the threat of hellfire and damnation in order to get their unruly classes to behave. Some parents might use the threat of "God's wrath" in order to get their way in a family. There are even some ethnic or cultural customs and traditions that use religious ideas to control others and maintain order rather than help them grow. Sometimes we have to separate what is Catholic from what is merely family dynamics or ethnic culture. God's voice can never be used to coerce, control, or manipulate. After all, we are free and equal to each other. We know religion is used at times for these nonreligious purposes. We certainly don't have to follow them. Nothing can interfere with our Garden virtues of freedom, equality, goodness, and service.

However, if we hear those voices repeatedly, and especially in many emotionally intense experiences as young children, they can become harder to ignore. A harsh voice of criticism at that young age can often be interpreted as *"I am bad"* rather than *"I have done a wrong behavior."* Very young children do not yet have the wisdom to see the difference between behavior and identity. They can tend to equate wrong behavior with being a wrong person. That harsh message cannot be the voice of God for we were created good. That repeated negative voice has such a powerful impact over the years that we can tend to hear it automatically whenever our behavior goes against what others say is good. That is unhealthy guilt. Unhealthy guilt says that our very self is bad. We certainly don't have to listen to a voice like that.

However, that voice is so hurtful that some people will shut out all voices completely as a defense. *They will tolerate no comments about their behavior.* They will claim only themselves as judge for what they do. They will let no one comment on the choices they make. That defensive voice will rationalize and easily minimize sinfulness. For example, we hear that voice often today saying something like, "What's the problem! Everyone does it now. It's no big deal anyway. Get over it! We're in the new millennium!" We cannot listen to that defiant voice either, for only God knows the good. While the fear of critical judgment is understandable, the defiant reaction is worse. Just like Adam and Eve, we shouldn't set ourselves up as the final judge on what to do or what is good. Ironically, we have nothing to fear from the person who counts the most, our Father in heaven.

The healthy person doesn't fear to acknowledge guilt because of a deep belief in the Garden of Eden Virtues. They *know* they are free, equal, especially good, and helpmates to each other. They know of God's *encouraging* love. No one can tell them any different, and no one should! Therefore, it is without fear that they can freely and easily acknowledge their faults. *They know these sins will be a source of learning, growth, and maturity.* They will learn to put them behind, learn from them, make the right changes, and move on to a happier life with renewed intentions to choose wisely according to the proven God-given way for happiness.

That inner voice of acceptance by God is too strong to be swayed by the crowd or anyone else, whether living or a "ghost" from the past. That inner voice is the source of strength and hope for the future. That is why the sacrament of confession can be so liberating. That is also why we *stand* at our full height at the very beginning of Mass when we confess our sinfulness in the Penitential Rite. We do not kneel or grovel or beat ourselves at that moment. In a beautiful sign of the *dignity* we have in the Lord, we *stand*. If He loves us, then so should we for ourselves. That is a voice of love we must listen to!

The healthy voice invites us to learn, grow, and mature. The healthy voice invites us to seek God's plan and His way of behaving. Our past mistakes can inspire us to study more, to seek the wisdom of God as He has already revealed it in His revelation. We can seek what church teachings, which are based on the traditions He handed to the church to safeguard down through the ages, have to say about various issues. Without fear we can safely let go of our past way of doing things, knowing that we will assume "the way" that will really lead us to a more fulfilling and satisfying life.

The longer we hear this affirming voice of God that calls us to growth, the easier it will be to acknowledge our own mistakes. Rather than avoiding confession, rather than avoiding the admission of our mistakes, we can eagerly take the time periodically to survey our behavior and measure it against the standards of the Lord. With a healthy confidence in God's love for us and a deep sense of our own goodness, we can without embarrassment and without shame acknowledge the truth about our behavior. What do we, of all people, have to fear? Certainly nothing from the Lord. Other people might be harshly judgmental, but not Jesus. After all, making mistakes says very little about our character. Admitting them and learning from them says so much more. While we can never condone sin or minimize its impact or deny its evil, it is what we do *after* the problem that more defines our character as Christian or not. That sense, or repentance, learning, and wisdom gained is the mark of the mature Christian. We will never be perfect, but we can at least be honest!

Returning to the Garden Virtues

The Garden virtues and the voice of healthy guilt help set a good and mature attitude toward God and the world. However, attitude is one thing; actual behavior is another. The next sections will take a more practical look at modern moral problems and how we can understand each as a point of balance between different forces that either help or hinder our Garden virtues. Moral problems invite us to seek what Jesus would do. Theories, attitudes, and high-sounding concepts don't help unless they help us where it counts, in everyday life.

Morality is balance. It is the balance first found in the Garden of Eden, where the right relationships were found between Adam and Eve and between both of them and God. That balance must be ours as well. We let God be God, and He respects our freedom to choose our own way in life. However, we believe God did design us in a certain and specific way. When we live that way, we are not only living morally but also living in the most natural way possible, the way we were designed. We then feel the most peaceful and fulfilled, for we are simply living according to our "manufacturer's instructions." We believe the moral life is actually buried deep in our very nature. If we put anything else in the place of God, such as drugs or selfishness or money, we have an imbalance, an unnatural state of things. If we put ourselves over someone else in a relationship of domination or force, we upset the balance of nature, or God's plan for the world. Choosing that imbalance is always wrong, for we cannot change the way we were made. *Treating a person as a thing is always wrong in all cases.* That happens whenever we offend against freedom, equality, goodness, or love. We should not change the way God designed the world or us. Morality is not that complicated, really. It is first seeing and then living the gifts of freedom, equality, and helping service that God put into the core of our nature as human beings. Let's see how this works in concrete situations.

Discussion Starters

1. Describe a person in your life who always encouraged you. What were the personality issues that you liked the most about that person?

2. How do you think God reacts when you commit a serious sin?

3. How does guilt feel to you? What makes you feel guilty?

4. What are your thoughts about good and bad guilt as explained in this chapter?

5. Describe some examples in which people are treated as objects or things. Do you believe there are behaviors that are always wrong in all circumstances? If so, describe a few of these.

CHAPTER 3

Relationships

Loving and Being in Love

Love is the center of the moral life; yet it seems so elusive to understand. People spend a lot of time wondering what it is, how to do it, and where to find it. It is only right that we start our discussion of morality by talking about love.

What is love? How do we know we really love someone? How can we tell we are not being selfish and really care for another? Ironically, we start our human life in an extraordinarily selfish way. We are born as needy and, quite appropriately, selfish babies and continue as fairly self-centered toddlers. We take and take from the world, from our parents, from our families, from everybody! After all, that is the way God made us: to take in quickly and learn as much as we can. With each year of maturity, however, the "taking" decreases, and the "giving back" increases. After receiving so much in our youth from our families, friends, and God, we begin to enjoy giving back and helping others enjoy their life. That actually defines the mature person.

What we receive as a gift, we give as a gift.

31

Maturity is that growing awareness we have of the needs of others while we develop and become persons ourselves. Simply put, we can ask ourselves a series of questions at the end of our day. "How much time did I spend wondering what I was getting in life today? How much time did I spend wondering how much I was *giving*?" For example, when I think of my family or friends, do I wonder first what can I do for them or what they will do for me?

Lovers are givers, not takers. Lovers enjoy giving more than taking, and they have no hidden agenda, ulterior motive, or secret game to play. There is no martyr or victim in love. A loving person already feels a sense of fulfillment and enjoys the time spent helping another enjoy life. That love is life giving. That kind of giving does not drain. There is no sense of loss—only the fullness that comes from a feeling of completeness in giving what we have first received.

What exactly is it that a loving person is giving? Certainly, it must be more than good advice, money, or expensive gifts, although a loving person would gladly give all of them when appropriate. What a loving person is doing when loving is *enhancing another person's experience of life just as Jesus did for us.* "I have come that you might have life and life to the fullest" (John 15:11). "I have come that you might have joy and joy that is complete" (John 10:10). Jesus always gave whatever enabled a person to grow, develop, mature, and feel fully alive. In that same spirit, a real lover does whatever needs to be done to bring the partner more joy and hope simply at being alive. He or she also encourages a partner to fully live all talents and abilities. Like the voice of God, a lover's voice is always and only encouraging and rejoices in the partner's accomplishments. A lover helps a partner be the full person he or she is called to be, the person that God meant him or her to be. A real lover would never use another to fulfill immature fantasies, cover personal inadequacies, or complete any other personal agenda. Of course, we believe that joy is deepest when life is lived as Jesus modeled. *When you simply enjoy and find great pleasure in doing these well-thought-out behaviors for another, you are loving.*

Sometimes people distinguish between love and being in love, with the latter feeling more unpredictable, free spirited, and fun. Being in love has a more "magical" notion to it that either happens or not. You just "click" with someone, or you don't. Well, it is important to give relationships the right name. Not all of them are love. For example, when an insecure person meets a strong and competent partner, he or she might instantly feel warm and wonderful feelings of safety and security. He or she might feel affectionate and call it "love at first sight." But that relationship might be more of a student-teacher or child-parent type than a partnership of free, good equals who are serving each other. The "click" that occurs most likely reveals that a more immature psychological need is being met rather than a decision to love and care. That is actually quite common at the start of relationships. We are naturally predisposed to find attractive people instantly who resemble early positive caregivers from our childhood. There is nothing wrong with that. But nostalgia is not love. Infatuation, admiration, hero worship, and sudden crushes are all relationships that can have many happy moments, but they are not love. Real love is the action of a mature and fulfilled person, not a half-person looking for the past or someone on whom to lean.

Love is a very mature decision that at times will include tremendous feelings of well-being and pleasure. After all, God wants us to love, so it is designed to be extraordinarily satisfying. In fact, it provides the deepest satisfaction of all. No wonder it is the quest of every person.

Finding a Partner to Love

Since Adam and Eve, we humans still seek each other as partners in life. What kind of person makes for a good partner is a question that has had different answers at different times. For example, today there is so much commercial emphasis on the external factors of persons, such as body measurements, dress, money, and job. These externals can distract us from the task of developing our inner self and our personality, of discovering something of who we really are, or of discovering whom the other person is. Focused on the outside, we can forget the inside. We can forget to develop a real sense of self for ourselves. If our identity is wrapped around externals, we'll have neither belief in ourselves nor enough confidence in our ability to start a relationship. No wonder the thought of meeting people can be so stressful. In those superficial meetings, our defenses go up, and role-playing replaces honest self-communication. It takes a lot of psychic energy to play a role but so little to be ourselves.

For centuries, arranged marriages addressed that problem by having the parents pick the partners. Sometimes they chose for love and the benefit of their children; sometimes they chose to improve the family business. Today, friends will often end up arranging marriages with the modern custom of "blind dates." Friends who know and like you and also know another good person they sense would be the most appropriate for you arrange for you both to meet. Your friends hopefully have the objective ability to match people based on clear thinking and not on pretense. Sometimes it works and sometimes not, but anything that helps an honest and genuine encounter is good. For example, gathering people in groups to do a common project, such as a sport, a charity event, or a business venture, helps lower defenses also. If the reason for gathering is the common project and not "meeting a date," then defenses are down and the "real person" has a chance to come forth. It is no accident that so many relationships begin at places of work or at school, where the reason for being together is a common project, without the need to impress a prospective partner.

Building a relationship and creating intimacy are a lot like playing cards. We want to begin a cycle of personal sharing with the other, and so we successively reveal deeper and deeper things about ourselves to the other, as if we were slowly playing more valuable or higher cards in a game. If the other returns the sharing in like manner, the experience can be quite thrilling as our intimacy grows. When the person still wants to keep sharing, even after the revelation of our weaknesses and faults, then the experience is even more satisfying.

Telling true stories about ourselves to another creates a very fulfilling experience of intimacy and closeness.

Intimacy is the main goal of relationships and can happen with a friend or a spouse. Intimacy is the feeling of closeness we have with another, and it is profoundly satisfying. That intimacy happens in the telling of true stories about ourselves to another and the other person doing the same with us. *Simply put, it happens by talking.* There can be no intimacy without talking and self-revealing. Even the common gender stereotype of the talkative female or taciturn man is no excuse for avoiding real sharing. In fact, excessive talking or quietness may be defenses against real communication, which is relating what is actually going on inside us. Intuition and guessing are also no substitute for talking. In fact, many problems develop from one person or the other thinking they "know" just what the other is thinking or feeling. Even if a couple has been together for many years, and even if their "hunches" are often correct, it is the actual act of articulating our innermost thoughts that engenders new and deeper levels of closeness. Relying on a hunch risks misunderstanding because it is based on how your partner has acted in the past. Maybe he or she has changed, and guessing would miss that. Without self-revelation there is no closeness. Sharing stories is crucial to intimacy.

In that intimate sharing, a couple explores their values and beliefs. Some values are just surface feelings or thoughts and do not mean very much. They may be merely life preferences, like enjoying movies or vanilla ice cream. Others are just a reporting on events, as in, "I went to the store today."

But the real intimate stories reveal our deeper *reactions* to events, as in, "I saw this remarkable event today, *and this is what it meant to me....*" Conveying the meaning of an event signals that the experience has been processed through our personality, intelligence, understanding, and view of the world. What meaning we get reveals our sense of ourselves in the world, whether it is hopeful, pessimistic, confused, or confident, to name just a few possibilities. The meaning we derive reveals our unique "take" on the world. Finally, some stories are even more central to us. These stories reveal our core values. These values are so central that we know we cannot be happy without them. They may be attitudes or beliefs about children, fidelity, careers, education, parenting, or faith. They may be what we think is the meaning of life itself. A couple that hopes to marry must know and have *compatible* core values. They don't have to be identical, but they cannot be in conflict, mutually exclusive, or contradictory. For example, a person who wants to have children and a person who wants more education have different but compatible core values. A person who wants many children and one who wants none have exclusive values. Differences in other areas can make for an interesting relationship that provides a couple with chances to practice compromise and dialogue. Different preferences can make for fun bantering, teasing, or friendly debate. Core values, however, must be shared or at least be compatible and cherished by both.

Sexual Morality

Sexual behavior balances our body and our mind with the body and mind of another. In other words, what we do with someone physically should match the relationship or balance with what we know and feel emotionally about that person. We know from our own experience that relationships grow through several levels of emotional intensity. Each level of a relationship has a natural physical expression or sign that matches or balances with it. A low emotional level matches a low-level sign. We can actually feel this balance very personally, again because it is part of our very own deep-rooted structure as human beings. For example, we tend to shake hands with people we have just met. We naturally sense that a mere acquaintanceship will match with a very simple physical sign such as shaking hands, while a deeper friendship will match with an embrace or a kiss. As the level of relationship increases and becomes more intimate, the physical sign becomes more intimate as well. For instance, two people deeply in love will kiss each other passionately. However, we believe the level of commitment comes first, before the physical expression. That is an important point. We believe sexual activity is an expression of a relationship or commitment *already given*. So what commitment matches intercourse? Well, we believe the highest commitment you can give another is to say these remarkable words, of which the marriage vows are a summary: *"I will love you and be faithful to you, and be faithful to you forever, and I will announce that to God and to the whole world so that others will also see the glory of God in our love!"* Those are the Catholic marriage vows. We believe no other combination of words says more. "There is no greater love than to lay down one's life for another" (John 15:13). A love that is received from God through another, given back freely to that person, and even shared with the whole world is the love God wants us to have because it provides the fullest and most satisfying experience of joy.

Because sexual intercourse is the highest form of physical expression, it simply makes good sense that it is matched with the highest personal commitment, which is marriage. That is why it simply makes sense that intercourse is reserved for people who have a married relationship. Church morality is not some arbitrary rule imposed by an unfeeling bureaucracy; it is actually deeply rooted in ordinary human experience, where God placed it. It is the way we are designed. Living that way will bring us the joy God intends for us.

We know some couples are tempted to express their love with sexual intercourse before marriage. They might even declare their love for each other quite often. However, they also might each have a different notion of what their love means, as well. Even worse, *they might not even know* they have different ideas about their relationship. For example, one might see intercourse as an intimate time, signifying great intensity of loving feelings, but only for that moment, whereas the other sees it as a more lasting promise of commitment. For one, it is a deep promise for the future, while for the other, it might simply be a great way to end an evening. They use the same word *love* and yet remain at very different levels of emotional connection. Without marriage, some couples may confuse each other about their intentions. At least the marriage vows are a commonly understood level of commitment—the very highest. When they say these words, their sexual life can become so much more natural, free, and satisfying. There is no confusion. Their sex life then expresses a level they both know and understand and to which they agree completely.

Sexual activity is really another form of talking. We say things with our body. Morality is really making sure our body-talk is clear and authentic and matches the God-given qualities of goodness, freedom, equality, and service. Our body-talk and our relationship must balance. As our bodies are "talking," our body-talk must also be received clearly by another. It must be a *mutual* conversation. As in any conversation, if the other person does not talk back or want to talk at all or is on another topic, then there is no communication. Body-talk must be clearly mutual. There is a balance between partners. Sexual activity makes the most sense when both agree on the message!

We know sexual behavior is highly emotional and is very close to our heart. Sexual activity is very personal and intimate. We become vulnerable before another. Any comments about sexual behavior must be respectful of everyone involved, especially because we often make mistakes, misunderstand each other, or get things out of balance. We want to call the mistakes by the right names and not overdo criticism. The word *sin* is at the same time an emotional trigger, perhaps recalling past hurts, and a great learning opportunity. We must use it responsibly in sexual behavior.

Sin is simply an imbalance. To the degree that there is a mismatch, or imbalance, between physical sign and emotional relationship is the degree to which the behavior is sinful or immoral or imbalanced. For example, for intercourse on a one-night stand, the imbalance is great, whereas among longtime lovers, the imbalance is somewhat less. For lovers, there is clearly more affection, love, and understanding but still not quite the full commitment that the sexual act *physically says* is there. Although much good might be present, such as affection and tenderness, there is still an imbalance because commitment is not. Of course, every act is always a mixed bag of intentions, motives, and purposes. No act is ever done for all good or all bad reasons but is always a mixture of both. In sexual behavior, it is good to know the proportions of each.

Morality helps us to see things clearly and honestly and in a healthy perspective. When we are thinking morally, it is easier to give relationships the right name. Not every romance that has affection and powerful feelings is necessarily love and commitment. Moral thinking helps us to see honestly the good that is present, as well as the good that is yet still not there.

Cohabitation

What about the couple that is committed and even engaged to be married? How should we look upon couples who live together before marriage? Does living together really help a couple prepare for a lifetime commitment? Does it make any difference? According to most sociological and psychological studies, there are several different reasons why couples cohabit today. Of course, some reasons are better than others. Obviously, if the reasons are related to parental rebellion or a desire simply to have sex without responsibility—or worse, to avoid commitment—then there is almost little or no chance for the subsequent marriage to be successful. Immaturity is immaturity, no matter where you find it, and it is certainly present in those reasons.

However, some couples choose cohabitation in a sincere desire to ensure compatibility and thus increase the chances of fulfilling a lifetime commitment. That is certainly a noble reason. However, it may be the wrong approach. Cohabitation may inadvertently be the wrong "tool" to use to improve commitment success. Even though they may have sincere motives to improve marital success, cohabiting couples may actually decrease their chances for a lasting union. In fact, a review of hundreds of professional psychological research studies during the last thirty years indicates interesting and robust results for the honest question of many young couples today, "What will be the effect of cohabitation on our future marriage?"

Marital outcome of prior cohabiting couples can be seen in two ways: *(a)* are couples who cohabited prior to marriage *happier*, and *(b)* do their marriages *last?* A review of almost all of these studies completed in the last thirty years indicates two clear results. Prior cohabiting couples have almost the *same* level of happiness and satisfaction as couples that did not cohabit before marriage. Cohabitation actually made *no difference* in marital satisfaction. Having the same level of happiness indicates that cohabitation does not affect the relationship one way or the other while the couple is together. We cannot say that it improves on the chances of success when it has actually no effect at all. Perhaps it was because their entrance into marriage was not a very radical change from their former life because they were already sharing a home.

However, the second result was even stronger. Divorce was definitely more likely for the prior-cohabiting couples. The ease of entering marriage perhaps makes the exit easy as well. Ironically, these divorces were often more amicable. Perhaps there was less of each person deeply investing himself or herself in the relationship, and so the desire to work hard to overcome troubles, difficulties, or trials was much less, as well. As long as things were going smoothly, then a prior-cohabiting couple was as happy as any couple. However, if any difficulties emerged, they were more likely to just separate and would do so more quickly and easily.

Cohabitation can accurately measure the ability of couples to be roommates and manage a house, but it turns out to be an unreliable tool for discerning commitment. Commitment implies a sense of dedication no matter what, and the ease with which a couple could exit during cohabitation can prevent the ability of each to discern the deep level of commitment needed for a lasting marriage. In fact, because the level of commitment is low, coupled with the public sharing of a home, there can be a reluctance between a couple to raise important questions or topics for fear that it will end what is, after all, a tenuous relationship. Cohabitation can actually stifle the level of communication needed to share core values and intimate talk. There is sometimes a certain kind of "hedging-a-bet" aspect to cohabitation that hinders the measurement of commitment. Ultimately, the only psychological factor that determines both good marital success and long marital duration is good old-fashioned maturity. Mature couples need only the time to talk honestly, openly, responsibly, and completely with each other to ensure a prediction of marital success.

Catholic Marriage

Our God-given nature reveals the secret of a happy life. When our life is about giving rather than getting, we can experience a deep sense of fulfillment and a profound feeling of joy. We are happy. Every vocation, whether it's priesthood, marriage, or single life, is happy when it is about giving. For Catholics, marriage is not only a private affair, but it also is a personal and public promise to God and your spouse to give and receive love for three very uniquely Catholic reasons: (a) to love your spouse totally and forever, (b) to experience *personally* the joy of the presence of God, who is all love, and (c) to be a public sign of the love of God *to others*. To want to inspire others to God's love in addition to having one's own experience of God is the highest form of love. *What we have received as a gift, we give as a gift.* "No greater love is there than

to give one's life for another" (John 15:13). All of that kind
of giving is expressed and promised at the marriage ceremony. No wonder people like to go to weddings! They
know they are seeing something powerful and rare. There is
a wonderful balance between the couple's need for love and
the community's need to see the presence of love in this
often-dark world.

In marriage, two become one, but it is the union of
two complete persons, not two half-persons. Very often, our
partners might be strong in areas we are weak. For example,
one might be outgoing, while the other is quieter. We cannot "use" the other's strength in place of our own talents or
in lieu of our ever developing them. Marriage is not an
excuse to stop growing in those areas in which our spouse
is strong. Instead, each partner can encourage the strength-
ening of those areas in which the spouse is weak. Each person then, encouraged by his or her spouse, develops fully
that gift of life received from God. A partner can help nourish those qualities but cannot replace or substitute for them.
Each person promises to enhance the joy, the growth, and
the development of each other. They promise to nurture the
Garden virtues in each other. Married couples encourage,
enhance, protect, and nourish all their common core values
for the rest of their lives.

A Catholic marriage includes many of the ideas in the
"Loving and Being in Love" and "Finding a Partner to Love"
section above. Catholic partners are mature persons sharing
and developing their compatible core values. As each person
is in the world to fulfill a unique role from God, so does each

marriage discover and fulfill its plan from God. After all, we believe that marriage is a "calling" or a vocation from God. Each marriage has an additional unique purpose besides the three listed in the first paragraph: "Two have become one" (Matt 19:5), so they also share a *common project* or purpose to fulfill. Just as each person has a plan to fulfill, so does each marriage. For many marriages, it might be the raising of a family, but it can also include a business project or important charity work or some other noble enterprise. Besides bringing great joy to a couple, a Catholic marriage helps to make the world a better place by its life of service to others. That is why the Catholic community places such a great emphasis on marriage preparation and understanding. We all have a stake in successful marriages.

Fidelity

People do not stay the same over time. Life is a moving river, and we cannot keep it still. People grow—they mature, get sick, move away, graduate from school, have children, are promoted or demoted, and, as always, grow older! Two people will not change at the same time or same rate either. Fidelity means we promise to stay with a person despite the changes. It assures that one will not move too far away without bringing the other along throughout the journey. Fidelity assures that the change is not a threat but will be worked out in dialogue with your partner. There is a good reason for this. It is difficult to see ourselves clearly and objectively, and we easily get things out of perspective. We can maximize or minimize events unfairly. Objective voices can help. The massive counseling and therapy worlds are testament to that. We need someone with whom we can bounce around ideas and work out our thoughts. Fidelity assures us that there will always be that person there for us, whatever the changes in our life. Making your vague feelings or ideas intelligible to a trusted person can finally make them intelligible to the most important person—you.

Fidelity steadies emotions. Feelings are elusive, unpredictable, powerful, and even overwhelming. Sometimes there is a rhythm to their ebb and flow. Romantic feelings rush in, slowly fade to disillusionment, and suddenly return as renewed passion. These emotions give relationships their fire. However, sometimes people panic at disillusionment and assume the relationship is over, only to be confused by the sudden romance. No relationship can be based on such a roller coaster of feelings. Love is more a thoughtful decision we make to stay with one person forever, despite the up and down feelings and the up and down changes. Fidelity is a decision and means the relationship is safe and secure, even if feelings have, for the moment, died down. Fidelity enables us to discover our fullest human potential and experience change, while keeping our feet on the ground—the ground of caring and honest dialogue. Fidelity steadies our emotional journey through life.

One of the greatest threats to fidelity is a weekly routine that may cause one or the other partner to take the relationship for granted. For example, a husband may forget to notice how his wife has changed since having a baby or going back to work or moving to a new home or passing a significant birthday. They may both quickly settle into routine housemaking chores that do not include talking regularly with each other as they did while dating. They forget to pay attention to each other and so drift apart. Fidelity is not a one-time promise. It must be renewed and revisited often with regular intimate talk.

Faithful couples make sure they schedule some time each week to share intimate conversation and stories about the meaning of their experiences. That way, they can always track the changes in each other, and before they change too much. They regularly "check-in" with each other's deepest feelings, needs, hopes, fears, and dreams. Perhaps they choose to walk around the block once a week, just the two of them. Fidelity encourages a couple to make that intimate talk *on a regular walk*. That ensures they remain attuned, attentive, and responsive to each other. That way, even after they are married, they stay "engaged" in the truest sense of the word.

Fidelity actually "occurs" at specific moments of temptation. These are "decision moments," when a person decides to remain true or not. It may be a dramatic temptation or a fleeting enticement, but each event can increase or lessen the level of commitment a person feels. If your partner knows about the temptation and your faithful response, it adds immeasurably to the trust in your relationship. That trust is like an account you share between yourselves and that you both add to from time to time.

Infidelity is a threat to the trust a couple has built over time. Breaking that trust is very serious and has ended marriages and broken apart families with consequences that can last for years, even for generations. Can trust ever be restored? Like any trauma, it depends on the intensity, frequency, and duration of the unfaithfulness. It also depends on the level of repentance, resilience, and recommitment in the couple. Repentance means the unfaithful person has stopped the affair and seriously and honestly looked at the causes and motives behind it. Resilience means both persons examine what was broken and measure their ability to recover. For some couples, a one-time, small event can be major, while for others, many events are taken in stride. Infidelity can mean different things for different people. This may be because different couples place the "center," or the core values, of their marriage in different places. It may not always, or only, be in sexual behavior. For some, it is in intimate sharing or time together or parenting. For others, it is all of them. What they consider their center, or core values, may not have been compromised, even though they might be core values of our faith. Honest sharing reveals what each considers the center of their relationship and if it were broken and how seriously. Recommitment involves healing and a couple's desire to start over again. Sometimes, a reconciled couple has a much stronger relationship than ever before. They have had to seriously recommit to each other *as they actually are now,* with a fuller knowledge of their weaknesses and strengths.

Infidelity is also a major theme throughout the scriptures, especially in the Old Testament. In story after story, God remains loyal and true, but the people often stray. Yet, in every event, God seeks their repentance and reconciliation.

He never stops loving them. Those stories reveal that unconditional love is possible, and we have the perfect model of faithful love in Jesus. Understanding that unconditional love is key to understanding our own marriage. His love can be a great comfort and an example for us in our relationship with our spouse.

Honesty and Lying

What does it really mean to tell the truth? We know the seventh commandment says "You shall not bear false witness against your neighbor," but does God expect us to *always* tell the truth, at *all* times, and in *every* case? Is it possible for any person today to always and only tell the truth? Is it ever okay to lie?

We know God made us *in His image,* so we have a fundamental dignity that makes us worthy of giving and receiving respect from *every* person. We can *never* do or say anything that infringes on that dignity. But to knowingly speak ill of someone, spread falsehoods, or tell lies about another does just that. We owe everyone the good name they have as a child of God, so we cannot speak in a way that falsely destroys that good name in the eyes of others. That is slander. But what if we speak an awful *truth* about someone, such as a past crime? Even then, we must speak of the sin, not the sinner; the behavior, not the fundamental dignity of the person. Words can be powerful weapons, so we must use them well.

God designed us be helpmates to each other. God made sure that no one could make it through life alone and be happy. We need people with whom we can talk intimately. We need people for assistance, to share experiences, to receive support, and to be there for us in difficult times. The intimacy and love we develop is based on the words and behaviors we say and do with each other, so we need to know they are real and true. After all, we cannot verify and prove everything ourselves, so we need to rely and trust in the word a person gives us. We cannot read each other's minds, so we must depend on their sincerity and that what they say is the truth. Telling the truth is crucial to the health and endurance of all our relationships.

However, it is difficult to know the truth of things and to know what the truth is. We cannot see ourselves objectively very well *by ourselves*. We are too close to our situation. Left to ourselves, we often get things out of perspective. We might minimize important things and maximize little things—all the more important to share honestly with each other. It is important to hear the truth from others as constructive feedback or to compare their honest experience of life with ours. This honestly shared experience of life brings us closer to the truth of the reality around us. Living in the truth of things, being connected to reality, and seeing things as they actually are, are forms of the very definition of mental health, that is to say, living in reality. Living amid lies and falsehoods is not. Jesus told us it is "the truth that will set you free" (John 8:32).

What about the "white lies" we feel obliged to use everyday? Aren't those words important also? Well, not everything we say to each other is that important. Sometimes we are just engaging in idle chatter or polite social talk. Someone might say, "How are you?" We respond, "Just fine, thank you" when actually we have a headache and feel terrible. We might tell others they are looking younger, have lost weight, or any number of little compliments that may not be true. These words are simply polite social interactions. They are not meant to be accurate medical or psychological inquiries or definitive character judgments. They are standardized rituals designed to make initial social interactions smooth and gracious. They provide the ground that makes more intimate and truthful talk possible as the conversation ensues. They are simply ways to start conversation that hopefully will become more authentic. They are not actually questions requiring rigid adherence to accurate and truthful responses. Everyone knows this, instinctively. We know there is no expectation of truth.

But how can we tell if a white lie is actually a white lie and not a more serious falsehood? We can ask ourselves, "What is the *expectation of truth* in this case?" What if the other person finds out the real truth? What will be his or her reaction? Will that person understand our kindness and thank us for it? Will the person understand our care and sensitivity for their feelings, or will the person feel betrayed or angry? What will be his or her expectation of truth? Did the person really just want a little politeness or really actually want and need accurate feedback? These answers can help us determine the morality of the white lie.

Can we lie in a more serious matter if it is for a good cause? For example, could you lie to a thief who asks where the money is stored in your home or business? Can a prisoner of war lie to conceal the whereabouts of fellow soldiers from the enemy? Does anyone have a right to the truth just because he or she asks? No. There is nothing requiring us to speak *at all* in such cases. We can certainly *withhold* sensitive information from dangerous people. The evil they might do is on their hands and never a direct consequence of our withholding. However, if we choose to speak at all, it would be wrong to lie. Helping others or any good end cannot change a bad action into a good one. The end does not justify the means. The importance of truthfulness in our speech, especially when there is an expectation and need for truth, is just too high. Of course, extreme emotional stress, the horrible threat of torture, the almost overwhelming desire to protect loved ones or important property, and other environmental factors can very much mitigate our personal responsibility, but they cannot change the rightness or wrongness of the action. We must still call the lie wrong.

Should you conceal a sin or an affair that has already ended from your spouse? Usually, that is the best course if several key issues are present: (a) The affair is over; (b) there is true repentance; and (c) all the proper lessons have been learned. That means there are no continuing issues affecting the marriage—just the wisdom gained by the penitent. If the situation involves anything that might still affect the present marriage, such as an acquired sexual disease, or childbirth, or some significant financial obligation, then the spouse needs to be told. If there are no continuing issues and the three key factors are present, then blurting out the story of an ended affair can be an unfair and heavy burden on an unsuspecting partner to understand the infidelity. Telling cannot be for the selfish purpose of making you feel better. All communication between spouses should help, not make matters worse.

Family Morality: Telling Each Other What to Do

The family is the place in which we first learn about life. It can be the best or the worst experience, so we should take the time to learn a few basic family dynamics. How spouses treat each other is so important for themselves and especially for their children. Here are two simple role-plays involving common family situations. They each bring out some of the original virtues God placed in us in the Garden of Eden.

One:

Wife: *"I need to talk to you now about our son."*

Husband: *"I'm reading now; let's talk after dinner."*

Wife: (angrily) *"You just don't think we are important at all!"*

Two:

Wife: *"What do you think of that TV actor you're watching?"*

Husband: *"He reminds me of our son."*

Wife: *"I agree. Let's talk about how he is doing."*

Remember: we were made in the image of God for freedom, equality, goodness, and service. These brief role-play dramas were meant to bring out the importance of freedom and equality in our own relationships, especially in those moments when we try to influence another in some moral behavior. While freedom and equality make real love possible and help in fulfilling our nature as helpmates to each other, we can forget them easily. Even though God placed *freedom, equality, goodness,* and *service* at the very center of our nature, we can place them somewhere else! We do so at great peril to our ability to communicate with those we love.

For example, because daily life is often stressful, we sometimes need to sit and ponder our situation and reorient ourselves. We need to think about things and what we are to do. After all, life presents a bewildering array of experiences to us, and they often come quite quickly and without a lot of time to react as we would like. It is not uncommon to come across people who are "lost in their thoughts" or pondering life's problems. We cannot read their minds, of course, and we cannot really know what is going on in another's head, but we do know from our own experience that we need those moments now and then to pull ourselves together and try to make sense of all that is happening. God gave our life to ourselves alone, and we'd better run it well! We might be thinking about the economy, our children's education, our neighbor's comments, or the last conversation we had with our spouse. Maybe even deeper thoughts might come to mind, like the very meaning of our life. In all these events, no one else can really know what is going on inside.

We take a great risk whenever we attempt to try. Most misunderstandings in relationships happen in this area of false assumptions. For example, we assume too quickly that our agenda must be more important than what other people are thinking at this moment. Therefore, we demand that they shift their attention to our area of thought *and that they do so immediately,* whether they want to or not. Assuming our agenda is better is the issue in role-play One, above. The wife assumed her story trumped anything her husband was doing. That is a risky judgment, and it just might be wrong. Any resistance is often taken personally or, worse still, as a statement about the value of our topic or of myself as a person. False choices are then set up. We say, "So! You don't think this topic (or me) is important! You think what you are doing is more important!" Communication breaks down.

In our God-given freedom, we have a right to think and have the thoughts we need. We must have that ability, for the proper running of our own life is primarily our own responsibility, and we must use our time well to reflect on it. We'd better make the time to do it right! Because we instinctively feel this right to think our own thoughts, we naturally resist any forceful attempt to commandeer our attention by force, especially if it is a sudden demand or a surprise command. Even if the person seems to be listening, the result is a poor communication connection. Have you ever finished talking to someone for a good period of time only to discover they haven't really paid any attention at all? That might be simply a natural resistance to your demanding his or her attention in a sudden or sharp manner.

In our God-given equality, we have no right to demand or command someone's attention against his or her will. Saying "Pay attention to me right now!" is a sure way to stop communication, for we cannot be other people's boss in this way. They may, however, voluntarily turn their attention over to us, and that is a fine and convenient thing to do, but we cannot demand that they do so. If they freely *choose* to give us their attention, then there is no problem and communication proceeds smoothly. It is important that we pay attention to where attention is paid.

Our God-given service calls us to help anyone in need, but we may not hear the need if our freedom and equality are ignored. The husband in the first role-play felt dismissed by his wife. Of course, one of the best ways he could use his gift of life would have been to offer it in service to others, especially his family. The best role-play scenario would see the husband immediately turn attention to this serious family matter. But we must remember that service is not service unless it is freely given. The role-play revealed the dynamics of his wife *interfering* with his free choice, not the goodness of her helping a son in trouble.

A person's thoughts are like a home that is private and personal. If we want to engage another person's mind, we had better take careful steps to enter that "home" respectfully. If we barge into it suddenly, we may be resisted *even if our message is wonderful and good.* The goodness of our message is no excuse to barge into the house uninvited and unannounced. For example, imagine you are sitting home alone late at night, perhaps even a little nervous about it, so you have a baseball bat nearby. Suddenly a man crashes through your front door. You hit him over the head, only to find out he is your neighbor rushing to report his house is on fire. Crashing into anyone's home late at night may get us attacked by an angry homeowner before he knows the goodness of our message. We must enter that home as we do any person's house, by being let in and never by force. Jesus always approached people with this same respect for freedom. We can follow a few simple guidelines to make our own entrance happen more peacefully and justly. Some may apply more than others, depending on whether you are at work, home, or with friends.

Knock first; announce your presence, especially if you are not well known.

"Hello, I am John Smith…"

Announce your intentions; why do you want to talk to this person?

"May I talk to you a moment about…"

Show respect by acknowledging the present activity of the person.

"I know you're busy, but…"

Acknowledge the other's right to refuse to talk right now.

"Is there a better time when we can talk about this?"

There are several sets of behaviors that can also make entry into another's world easier as well. We can call them the "Setup" and the "Slide-in" methods. They are not the only ways to accomplish connecting with another person, but they do acknowledge freedom and equality, and they acknowledge the difficulty of connecting with someone on challenging topics, such as moral behavior.

Setup You both agree on a time in the not too distant future to come together and discuss the issues. Set up an appropriate time and place for a full discussion in a simple but direct manner; for example, "I can sense this is not a good time right now. Let's get together after dinner on Wednesday evening in the kitchen and spend an hour going over this in detail. We can each say our piece on this topic and cover all the issues." (Then ask for a confirmation.) "Is that OK with you? Do you agree?" Both sides then have agreed to be on the same wavelength at the future meeting and even how they will discuss it. There is no need to forcibly "get" anyone's attention.

This setup time is an extremely powerful tool for growing or returning intimacy in relationships as well. In very busy lives, couples can forget to talk to each other when no crises or problems command attention. Ironically, the absence of crises can bring on a state of routine. Couples start to take each other for granted. They lose intimacy and closeness. They stop sharing their true intimate stories with each other. Remember: we believe intimacy grows by telling true, important, and deep stories about ourselves to another, with the other listening and responding in the same way. God designed us to grow closer together in care as we are drawn into the story of those we love. Wise couples schedule an intimate talk regularly, just like their dating time before marriage. Perhaps every week they would agree to spend an hour or so just talking about their relationship. Some couples like to do so while walking, say, around the block. It is their *intimate talk on a regular walk*. No distractions. No interruptions. The topic is only their relationship. That sharing keeps them attuned, attentive, and engaged. They ensure that there will be no "drifting" apart.

Precisely because we each want this intimacy so much, we can panic if we are not sure when we will be able to talk. That's why sometimes a partner will "pounce" the minute a spouse walks in the door and demand dialogue about some important topic, no matter what the partner is doing at that moment. However, if a partner knows there is a *guaranteed time* for sharing coming soon, there is no need to panic. More importantly, a partner's refusal to share immediately will not be taken personally or as a threat to the relationship. After all, the "Setup" date will happen soon.

Even God uses a "Setup" date with us. God knows we are all busy, preoccupied, and distracted much of the time. Yet, there is no need to panic because we have our "date" coming soon—on Sunday. Then God will tell us His most intimate story, the story of Jesus, and we can tell Him our most personal story in prayer. Sunday is our guaranteed time to grow in intimacy. Obviously we can pray anytime, but Sunday is our prearranged time, on which we have both agreed, to be intimate with each other.

Slide-In This is the example given in the second role-play, above. The wife *comments on a present activity* (watching TV) in a way that invites a response and is also along the lines of the desired topic. These interactive comments are extremely powerful learning events. They are actually the very way we learned things as toddlers and very young children. Attentive parents at times will comment on what their toddlers are doing at the moment. For example, they might say, "Do you like that red toy? Do you want to see what is on the table?" In this approach, you capitalize on what the child is *already interested in*. No need to control their thoughts away from something else; just use the area of attention where it is already focused.

Using the events of life as they are actually lived at the moment by the persons themselves is extremely effective. In fact, it was a principal method that Jesus used in the Gospels for teaching. He used the immediate concrete moment to bring out a lesson. For example, while walking in the countryside with His followers, many of them farmers, He stops and says, "Notice that farmer sowing seed in the field" (Matt 13:3). No need to command attention when it is already engaged.

Both of these techniques keep the conversation going in ways that affirm our Garden virtues. They both acknowledge the difficulty of actually connecting with other people and the problems inherent in human communication. They both take advantage of the ways that God made us to ensure that people actually communicate what is important. That enables intimacy to grow, and that is one of the things we find so satisfying about human relationships. Communication keeps a family together and makes possible healthy parenting.

Purpose of a Family

"I must be about my Father's business!" (Luke 2:49). Jesus said this to his parents while still a young man. He was twelve years old—the age of maturity in ancient Israel. After visiting the temple in Jerusalem, his parents started home for Nazareth, having accidentally left without him. Three days later, Mary and Joseph found him in the temple engaged in conversation with the leading teachers there. Mary expresses concern, tinged perhaps with a little reproach to Jesus arising from her own anxiety at wondering where he might have been. "Did you not know we have been looking for you these last three days?" Jesus responds with this remarkable reply turning her phrase around again to her, "Did *you* not know that I must be about my Father's business?" Jesus, the recently turned adult, declares the purpose of a family and of each person. Every person is to fulfill his or her destiny from God and from Him alone. A family is meant to enhance that destiny. A family provides safety, protection, and care so that each child in it can be *propelled* outward into the world to fulfill God's plan for him or her. Parents do not "own" their children. They have the temporary charge of "foster caring" for persons who always belong to God. That is why the responsibility of parenting is so strong. Every parent has God to answer to if a child is maliciously harmed, traumatized, or hindered from completing his or her mission.

The behavior of family members is important. In fact, it is the main thing that counts. One day while Jesus was preaching to a crowd gathered inside a house, word came that his family was outside looking for Him. This was a society in which "family" and family connections were everything. The implication was that He was to go with them. Jesus looked around the room and said, "Who is my family? Those who do the will of my Father in heaven!" In other words, "You don't tell me who my family members are. I tell you who they are, and they are those who *act* like family!" We are surrounded by so many titles in families: mother, father, brother, and sister. Jesus redefined them. He also redefined "neighbor" in the parallel story of the Good Samaritan. Both stories reveal that *behavior* is everything. In a real family, *mother* is not a title. It is an activity. *Father* is not a title. It is a behavior. A family is made up of people who act as family. A family consists of those people we love and who love us as God loves. Prior to adulthood, a child is generally obedient and respectful to all older persons in the family, especially the parents, in all appropriate matters. However, once a child becomes an adult, then all the adult members in a family become fellow peers. There is always a relationship of respect but no longer one of obedience.

Family Discipline: Telling Children What to Do

Every child will disobey a family rule at some point. What does a parent do next? How can parents tell children what to do in a way that respects the dignity and freedom of both? How can they avoid falling into power games with each other? Can parents avoid using force and fear with their children and still be good teachers of Garden virtues? Discipline is important, but if not done well, the entire family may suffer great unhappiness, right in its own home, which is supposed to be a place of encouragement and growth. At some point, parents must seriously discuss together the use of discipline in their family.

Discipline need not involve anger, exasperation, or sorrow. Discipline need not be heartbreaking, either. "Heart breaking" is the right image too. We often speak of the *heart* when we mean "emotions and feelings," just as we use *head* to mean "thinking and thoughtfulness." As children, and especially as babies, the heart ran everything in our life. As a baby, we were largely a little bundle of feelings, reacting to everything in highly emotional ways, such as crying or laughing. However, we soon realized that just emoting didn't always bring us what we wanted. That frustration inspired and motivated us to use our head to think of other ways to get our needs met. Maturity develops as the "head" process of thinking takes over from the heart. The many conflicts and challenges we face in life build our character and personality battle by battle. But problems develop when the heart remains too long in charge of behavior. The head must rule the heart in deciding on actual *behavior*. Even so, it shouldn't silence the heart or suppress feelings or deny emotion. It doesn't *lose* emotions; it *uses emotions* as a kind of fuel to give the head's decisions power and force.

We can well imagine the strong feelings our Lord had in the presence of the Pharisees, who were always giving

Him trouble. Yet, He *used His emotions* for courage to tell them stories of humility and service with a power and authority greater than theirs. We can too. For example, the anger I feel at some comment from another about my appearance can fuel my decision to lose weight or to practice better grooming. Connecting an emotion to a head decision also gives it more lasting power and effectiveness. If we associate any positive feeling we want to have (like looking good) to any difficult decision (like losing weight), we give the decision more strength and durability. By associating a pleasant memory of emotions from a past victory to some present decision in a difficult situation, we can make that decision easier to fulfill. Jesus used His love for the Pharisees to fuel His courage to challenge them.

The head and the heart each have a role to play, and good family discipline must use both in the right way. After all, children often act more out of their heart and strong emotions than their head. They may be afraid, angry, confused, or sad. They are not the ones you want in charge. Parents are just the right ones to bring balance. Parents must use their heads to decide on family boundaries and rules and use their hearts to provide the emotional fuel, energy, and courage to keep themselves steady.

Successful families set good, thoughtful, and healthy boundaries for themselves. Even though children often fight them, they actually provide a soothing sense of security. In fact, the rebellious antics of children are sometimes a behavioral search for the limits of acceptable conduct. They will keep "pushing the envelope" until they find a limit. They feel soothed by finally finding that boundary. After all, children don't know a lot about the world, which can seem big, unsafe, and frightening. They like to know someone is watching out for them. That is what boundaries do: provide that calming sense of protection. When children have no boundaries, or they feel uncertain, they will look for limits somewhere else. Ironically, one place that has some of the strongest rules of any social group is the urban street gang. Children from chaotic homes will find the structure they crave in amazingly strict gang rituals, clothing styles, and values.

Boundaries, or rules of discipline, in a family are like the guardrails on a very high bridge. With the rails, we feel comfortable to drive in our own lane right at the speed limit. However, without the rails, we tend to hug the center of the bridge and slow down, even though the road remains the same size. Boundaries provide security and freedom. Deep down, all people, and especially children, desire boundaries. They signal care. Discipline communicates interest, care, love, and protection. Good boundaries enable children to explore, discover, and reach out to the world. They communicate that the parents are putting the child's welfare above their own agenda and needs. That is the head over the heart again.

Children can have many symbolic meanings for parents. Children can symbolize a final break from their own parents, a feeling of importance in being needed, a chance to correct mistakes in their own life, or little people they can control and mold to their will. However, children are not the possession of parents; they are simply on loan for a while from God. We must remember that all people are created with the

Garden of Eden Virtues of freedom, equality, goodness, and service to each other. All people ultimately belong to God. Because of this awesome responsibility, parents should especially rely on the wisdom of the head in disciplining and not the heart and should make sure that all rules protect the Garden virtues of our children. They are in our hands that we might help them become autonomous and independent persons and to be helpmates to each other.

What if children misbehave? What if they go out of control? Parents become so exasperated at times trying to exert their will "over" their children. Everyone feels frustrated and angry. Is it possible to discipline children without rage or desperation? Whenever a child misbehaves, it is practically impossible for any parent to not take it personally. In fact, anytime *anyone* defies, it is easy to take it too personally, but it hurts especially to see our own child challenge our guidance. We might become depressed at this, or angry, perhaps even lose our temper. Maybe we even feel like striking back in revenge. This is precisely *not* the time we should be trying to think of what discipline to impose. Never try to think of discipline in the midst of hurt, angry, or confused feelings. Who knows what outrageous things we might say or do? Of course, anger is a natural human emotion and so a part of life that children must experience and come to understand, both in themselves and in others. However, it carries an especially powerful force when inappropriately expressed within a family, which is the source of so much power to shape our personality. With intense anger, we run the risk of adding other negative psychological factors to the event. For young children, out-of-control anger may call into question the relationship itself. For example, when a very young child hears out-of-control rage from parents, he or she might think, "I did something wrong, I am a bad person...and now I will be kicked *out of the family*!" That may seem silly or ridiculously extreme, but then again, this is a child thinking as a young child does, which is largely through feelings that are often irrational. We know, of course, that our anger is passing and only expresses our disappointment. However, children are young and immature and so cannot know for sure what the anger means, or even how long it will last.

There is a way to provide for less emotional discipline and to lessen the chance that discipline will degenerate into a power contest or a test of wills between parents and children. After all, we want to respect the Garden virtues of everyone. However, it is a system that is meant to set healthy boundaries only for *the most important areas* in your family's life. Keeping things simple is a good way to start.

This is not a new idea. Jesus changed the 613 laws of the scriptures to just the three most important: Love God, love your neighbor, and love yourself. He funneled the whole law down marvelously to the most basic and important rules. In the same way, your main family rules should be only the five or ten behaviors that you feel are the most necessary for your family to live in peace and that will provide for family growth. They are the most important ones that you simply don't want to live without in order to have peace and to help children learn to do good. The simplicity of Jesus is a model for family discipline. He is simple, loving, and yet wonderfully firm.

Every good discipline system includes some *code* and some natural or logical *consequences* applied with love. Code and consequence should follow naturally right on the other. The code describes desired behavior, and the consequence reveals results. Consequences are never meant to be punishments. They are teachings about life, in a way. They should be the *natural* results of bad behavior. For example, a red-hot stove is a good metaphor for this system of family discipline. Although everyone at some point has mistakenly touched a burning stove, we rarely burn ourselves *a second time.* The natural consequence or result has been learned well. Burning teaches clearly! There are five simple ideas that summarize this dynamic, and they easily prevent anyone from ever touching the stove again. These hot-stove rules will help ensure that your family's five or ten most important rules will be followed quickly and with little or no anger, rage, or loss of temper. A code of behavior must be:

Clear. A hot stove is *visible.* It glows red so you can see it is hot from a distance. Family rules must also be known, visible, and seen ahead of time by everyone. They could be posted on the refrigerator or some other central place. They could also be comments made to a child *before* going to a restaurant, church, or other public place. They are clear and unambiguous. They are also only about *behaviors that are easy to measure,* such as no hitting, no lying, an 11:00 P.M. curfew, no stealing, homework done and checked by 6:00 P.M., or cleaning your room by 8:00 A.M., and so on. Avoid unclear rules, like making something "neat," or wearing "good" clothes, or "being nice." Those are qualities that are difficult to measure and can be ambiguous. Again, try to have no more than ten. Five is about right. Choose carefully! Choose the most important behaviors you feel you must absolutely have in the house that help everyone live the Garden virtues.

Constant. A hot stove burns *everyone*. Family rules must apply to everyone involved. Of course, you can have different rules for different age groups in the family, but no one is above his or her part of the family code. Here, parents can be a great example. Your credibility skyrockets when you also live by rules. After all, God sent His Son to the world to live our life, even unto death. His Word became credible by sharing in our same human experience (John 3:16).

Consistent. A hot stove *always* burns when touched. Family rules must apply each and every time. Do not let an event pass by one day and then enforce it the next. To enforce a rule just now and then teaches everyone to ignore the rules—and eventually you! This is probably the worst kept rule, and not keeping it causes the most problems. If you are always repeating commands, you have probably taught your children to ignore you by that inconsistency. Being consistent especially helps remove wild or out-of-control emotions from the application of discipline.

Contemporaneous. A hot stove burns *immediately*. Don't wait a long time before you act on misbehavior. Discipline is either immediate or never. That allows the matter to be ended once and for all. Waiting fosters resentment, fuming, or sulking as the feelings about the infraction fester. Waiting also teaches a child to ignore you until you lose your temper. Unless the setting is public, it is usually best to deal with misbehavior right away. Bringing in past history is usually not effective. If you missed an opportunity, well, it's over.

Cooperative. *Every* hot stove burns. In two-parent families, both parents need to decide *together* on rules and to *support each other.* With that cooperation, children will not be able to play one parent off the other. Only the fully agreed upon rules by both parents are used. There should also be no surprise rules that children or your partner find out about later. Choose the rules very carefully and only after a lot of thought has gone into them. Check with other families for some ideas, but stick with ones that you want for your family and that you both will enforce. You are the ones who will live with them. You are the ones in charge!

When a child breaks one of the family rules, it might cause you some distress, disappointment, or even a little anger. That is certainly normal and expected. After all, perhaps your child broke a rule that was for his or her safety. Maybe you are distressed that your child has possibly endangered others. If it was a sudden shock or a very unexpected surprise, there is a higher chance of your losing your temper too. In the midst of that confusion, we can simply put our feelings aside *for a moment* and proceed to the refrigerator or wherever the family rules are kept and read the appropriate consequence. The rules have "done the thinking" ahead of time for us about what consequence to announce. If done in a loving, friendly, or simple manner, the child senses that there is "nothing personal" about the discipline. It is a natural but firm consequence of their own choices and not a comment on their personhood. The child also sees that there is a family "plan" or "way of doing things" for these events and that the parents are secure and in control. Of course, your child probably won't be happy with the consequence, but at least the event will not be contaminated by rage or violence. Afterward, you can express your anger in another place or talk things over with your partner, who as a fellow adult can help you make sense of it all.

What is applied in each rule is a natural or logical *consequence,* not a punishment. That is so important, for there must be both accountability for behavior and a system of teaching about life. Spend a good amount of time reflecting on the appropriate consequences for each child as you compose each family rule. Consequences are best when they are natural or at least logical. Rather than imposing a disconnected or arbitrary event, such as a monetary fine, let life's natural consequences or results work for you. For example, if a teenager does not get up on time in the morning, he or she may miss the already agreed upon breakfast period or the ride to school. No anger is expressed, no preaching occurs, no punishment is imposed, but the ride or meal is gone. If children misbehave in a public place, such as a restaurant, they may not go back there again until they show they can behave well. A parent may choose to clean *only* those plates or clothes that are left where they are supposed to be. Desired activities, like sports or play, are allowed only after chores are done. These are quiet, natural, or logical results of children's behavioral choices, not arbitrary impositions by the parents.

They allow the child to make choices and to learn to exercise wisdom. For example, in the case of the teenager above, no one "makes" a child get up in the morning in a test of wills. Instead, the child can choose to take advantage of breakfast and a ride to school or not.

Besides being natural or logical, consequences should share all the same qualities of clarity, constancy, consistency, and contemporarity and *always* require parental cooperation. While the family rules are public, sometimes it is best for the consequence to be private. That is not always possible, but discipline is usually better when kept within the family in a private setting, rather than imposed through a public scene that could add shame to a simple discipline event.

The moment of disobedience is still difficult for any parent. Many children become kind of minilawyers when caught breaking a rule. They become amazingly clever, even delightful and humorous, at using language to twist, distract, obfuscate, or confuse the situation, all for the purpose of getting out of trouble. That is certainly understandable (sometimes even charming) because it is a natural reaction for young people to avoid bad consequences. In fact, it is one of the definitions of immaturity. However, parents may possibly also become confused because of swirling emotions or the unexpectedness of the event or the cleverness of the excuses. After all, you weren't planning on a full-blown explanation for the laws of the universe just because the homework wasn't done! Parents can become especially irritable if they are hurt by the infraction. Tempers can flare as they become exhausted at trying to follow the labyrinthine arguments of a desperate child who is only seeking escape from a negative consequence or who is having fun at the parent's expense. There is a "magic" word that can help keep you steady and focused. When the child offers excuses, simply say, "nevertheless," as in, "Nevertheless, you will have to do this chore now." It is a word that does not deny their arguments or defend yours. It avoids a power struggle. It simply states that the rule applies and that the consequence follows anyway.

"Nevertheless" signals that the discipline is not mean spirited. After all, the consequences were already known. Nothing is new here, and nothing is personal. You are simply insisting the child follow what was already the plan. Most important, it helps you stay focused and keeps your emotions in check.

All of us take discipline best when it comes from someone who we know loves us and has our best interests at heart. We "give" or allow that person some control of our behavior. We let that person become a trusted "partner" in our responsibility for our own life. Discipline is so much easier in families when our children see us as three-dimensional real persons rather than as one-dimensional autocrats. They will "give" us their attention more. We become three-dimensional when our children come to know us more deeply, and that means telling appropriate stories about ourselves. They may be stories of significant conflicts we experienced and how we met and overcame them or happy memories of great joy. They may be happy or sad, but they are stories that invite intimacy and closeness in the family. If the only voice our children hear is a nagging voice that just announces consequences, then discipline will be tough.

Children naturally want to belong to their family. As they grow older and develop abilities, they also feel a growing need to contribute something to the home and to accomplish things on their own. They want to do good things. Parents can use that desire for good by praising their child's actual good behavior. Never miss an opportunity to praise, but only praise real accomplishment. Parental praise, plus children's sense of real accomplishment, helps build their self-esteem. Praise without accomplishment comes across as a kind of meaningless flattery, and children eventually sense and dismiss it. Accomplishment without praise may cause a child resentment and lead him or her to lose heart in further activities. Praise, accomplishment, and personal revelation are the ingredients that together foster self-esteem and intimacy. They are what children want and need, and they make discipline so much easier!

Divorce and Remarriage

"What God has joined, let no one divide" (Matt 19:6). Those are strong, clear, and direct words from Jesus Christ. So how is it possible for couples to divorce and remarry? Well, when two Christians marry, we presume they are marrying as Jesus would, and His love for us was always faithful, creative, and enduring. That means both partners promise to stay faithful, stay married forever, and be open to the possibility of new life. For Catholics, it also includes having their vows witnessed by a priest and two witnesses. We believe God wanted married couples to experience His love and grace in a special and *visible* way, so we call marriage a *sacrament,* an event God chooses that reveals His spirit in a way that appeals to our senses, like water in baptism or bread and wine in the eucharist. Marriage is a shared life of commitment that reveals to the couple and all who know them the same love God has for all of us. Of course, we cannot make a presumption of Christian intentions for non-Christians ,so their marriages are called valid but nonsacramental.

However, while we sometimes focus on the last part of the verse, "let no one divide," we cannot ignore the first part, "what God has joined." Not every couple enjoys a marriage that God intends. Of course, anyone can say vows in a wedding ceremony, but just saying them is not enough to make them valid. Sometimes, one person is mature and intends all that God intends for marriage, but the other person does not. Sometimes one partner can be in mortal danger of violence from the other, or there is a real threat to personal or emotional safety. Sometimes no amount of counseling can reconcile these dangerous situations. The church understands the need for couples to separate at times and even seek the legal protection of divorce. Whereas legal divorce does not actually break the marriage bond, the church does acknowledge the ending of a shared life together and the protection of legal rights and responsibilities, especially those regarding child support and alimony. The divorced person is still a full member of the church and is able to receive the sacraments, except of course for holy orders and marriage until the first marriage is resolved in some way. However, no matter how necessary, almost every divorce is painful. It represents a shared dream, once deeply held, that will never happen. Every divorced person should receive the presumption of having good intentions and our good will.

As always, we take seriously Matthew 19:6, "What God has joined, let no one divide," so we start with the presumption that God continues to affirm the marriage vows of the divorced couple even though they are separated. Before there can be a Catholic remarriage, the prior marriage, if between baptized people, is presumed sacramental and must be declared null or, if between nonbaptized persons, is presumed a valid nonsacramental marriage and must be dissolved. That happens in either the Declaration of Nullity or the dissolution processes. A valid and nonsacramental union may be dissolved according to the teachings of St. Paul in 1 Corinthians 7:12–15. No matter what the title, both processes attempt to reconcile the marriage with the words of the Lord in Matthew 19:6, "What God has joined, let no one divide."

Why are these Declarations of Nullity or dissolutions required? Well, Catholics believe deeply in the power of a promise kept. We believe in that power because it reveals God's relationship with us. God keeps His word, and so must we. That is integrity. When words and behavior match in a couple, they reveal a profound integrity that can have a powerful impact on others. That is part of its sacramental nature—its *visibleness.* It is one way people come to experience God: through the love of others. Marriage vows are the permanent promises we make to God, our spouse, and the church community. We take them seriously and at their face value of permanence, *unless it can be shown they were faulty in some way.* The process of finding if there was some fault that prevented the fulfillment of those vows is the Declaration of Nullity process. It looks for clear and visible signs that the vows were defective from the very start of the union. Visible signs could come from the statements of witnesses, marriage counselors, and documents, as well as the testimonies of the spouses. It looks not to place blame but to discover the truth before God of the reality of the marriage.

Both the Declaration of Nullity and the dissolution procedures are meant to be spiritual programs of this discovery process. Each involves the mutual discovery by the church, and the petitioner and respondent, of the couple's and God's intentions in this union. Did God intend for this couple to be married? Did this couple intend to marry with the intentions and abilities that God wants for Christian marriage? Both partners must have those abilities and intentions. If either partner lacks them *from the beginning* of the marriage, then the marriage can be declared null. Every marriage has problems, but not all of them are grounds for nullity. For example, if a problem occurs much later in the marriage, it may be grounds for counseling, separation, or even legal divorce but may not be grounds for nullity. Regrettably, it could be the "worse" part of "for better or worse." Of course, any children of this marriage are legitimate both in the eyes of the church and civil society. Children are always welcome in the world by the church and remain legitimate.

A Declaration of Nullity accepts that the marriage also was legitimate but not what God intended a marriage to be.

After a Declaration of Nullity, a person may remarry in the church. Of course, care must be taken that any of the original problems of the first marriage are no longer present for the one who wants to remarry in the church. Remarriage without a Declaration of Nullity or dissolution does *not* incur excommunication. But it does mean that a Catholic remarried person would not be able to receive the sacraments, except of course, the anointing of the sick in emergencies. This is not a punishment. It simply retains the consistency of the visible signs of sacramental love and that each sacrament visibly reveals the fidelity of God. Despite the legal divorce, the prior marriage bond remains unless there is a reason to see it otherwise. Forming a new visible bond with someone else acts against that first bond, which promised commitment.

What about dating a new partner after your divorce but before the Declaration of Nullity is finalized? This is a sensitive area. Obviously a divorced person should socialize by starting and maintaining friendships. That is simply the way God made us. But how dating occurs is important. Dating can mean different things to different people. It can mean ordinary socializing, or it can mean socializing *for the purpose* of finding a marriage partner. Obviously, some situations are more romantically powerful than others, so care must be taken to be honest about what is being communicated by our actions, not only to our dating partner, but also to others. Obviously, the opinions of others should not dictate our actions, but they should not be simply dismissed either. How you approach dating friends after a divorce demands a lot of self-honesty from both partners. We have to acknowledge honestly that the first bond still exists, so it would not be fair to seek a marriage partner while uncertainty remains as to whether the first marriage will be discovered to be null.

All of these events—marriage, divorce, Declarations of Nullity, dissolutions, remarriage—are all about honesty before the Lord and about what is actually true and real in our relationships. Each event demands integrity and facing the truth about our lives before the Lord. Did we mean these vows when we said them? Were they valid? What is God's will here? Must I remain faithful to my promises? All of the church's processes are about discovering and living in the truth. None of it is meant to be bureaucratic, harsh, or limiting. They are about freedom. "Then you will know the truth, and the truth will set you free (John 8:32).

Birth Control

In marriage, a couple makes a promise for complete self-giving to each other with no holding back. They *encourage* and *protect* for themselves and each other all of the Garden qualities of freedom, equality, goodness, and service, and they do so everywhere in the relationship. Because intercourse is a sign of that commitment already given, it expresses in one powerful action all that marriage is. Sexual behavior focuses in a few intense moments all those powerful feelings and promises but uses the language of the body.

Sexual activity is really another form of talking or giving with no holding back either. What do we say with our bodies in intercourse? What do we want to give our partner? Perhaps you could make your own lengthy list. Along with the Garden virtues and others such as honesty, trust, understanding, forgiveness, tenderness, challenge, and commitment, we believe we also give openness to new life.

Of course, we are only human, and we cannot perfectly give all of these gifts completely all the time. Sometimes at the end of the day, we are just too tired to be as caring or understanding as we would like to be. Some people may not be capable of being open to the possibility of new life because of medical reasons or old age. We all know how easy it is to forget during the week to give some of the many signs of love to our partner. However, we must not *consciously or directly refuse* to give any one of them either. To forget is one thing; to directly remove is another. For example, during intercourse, it would be just as unbalancing to refuse the tenderness or understanding of your partner as it would be to refuse to be open to life. We wouldn't say, "Tonight, I will be tender and kind and understanding, but I will not be honest or faithful." Directly choosing to remove something we can and should give is unbalancing. It is certainly startling when related to some of the other gifts we like to offer in marital love, such as tenderness and understanding. However, if the giving spirit is not there by direct and conscious choice, even if for a good reason like family planning, then it makes sense that we just don't do the act *that expresses that kind of giving.* That is the meaning of abstaining for family planning reasons.

Of course, family planning is a good thing and is often necessary for the well being of couples and families. How we go about it is important. We cannot practice infanticide or murder as some cultures advocate. Contraception actually involves two decisions. One is to have sexual intercourse; the other is to remove the possibility of new life from it. However, by not choosing the first, by choosing to abstain from sexual intercourse, the second choice of direct contraception becomes moot.

Natural Family Planning, or NFP, is simply a method that accurately and naturally monitors each woman's cycle, as erratic as it might be, and indicates by direct observation of one's own physical symptoms when fertile times begin and end. Couples can use NFP to either conceive a child or postpone conception. It is a unique form of family planning in that it requires both husband and wife to cooperate in the method. It cannot become just the woman's or the man's responsibility. It also is a method that allows a couple both to affirm their life-giving power given to them by God and to refrain from exercising that power for important family-planning reasons.

Certainly, any kind of abstinence brings on some kind of hardship for couples in that it infringes on the good effects of spontaneity in relationships. We tend to think very highly of spontaneity and don't like anything that blocks it. However, we are actually quite used to it. For example, people usually go to work each weekday, often separating from each other for ten hours or so, depending on work schedules and commuting time. That certainly infringes on spontaneity! Yet, the value the couple places on the food, clothing, and shelter that work provides actually helps them to encourage the separation. Work has a deeply held shared meaning for them—for example, the future security of their family—and so they will delay family time and sexual time until later. They want to preserve the good effects that their work provides. While spontaneity is good, we are very used to letting it go for even higher values. This is not a new skill for couples. They are used to it.

Family time together may be more difficult to schedule with work demands and may take on even added speciality because of its rarity, but we still delay it for the greater value of family financial security. Lovemaking can also share in that difficult-to-schedule situation, and its occasional delay can also be for that same value of marital security. However, if a couple does not share the same values about work or children, then work or NFP could be seen as a threat.

Delaying intercourse also occasionally can encourage couples to rediscover, develop anew, or perhaps cherish again the whole range of intimate sexual behaviors that are often too quickly brushed over in favor of intercourse. Couples can add to their "vocabulary" of body-talk and invest so much more powerful meaning in the simple acts of holding each other, embracing, and caressing. Occasional abstinence can encourage couples to become "experts" in lovemaking for they will learn to express their love in so many new and stimulating ways.

It also means their lovemaking will be so much more consciously willed and therefore so much more personally intended, rather than being a mere whim or a sudden instinct. After all, who wants to be the target of an instinct? Knowing that a time of lovemaking has been longed for, prepared for, and sacrificed for can add to its intensity. Knowing that *you* are the one longed for is so much more special than being the object of a whim or, worse, simply being the nearest handy person! We all want love for us to be, well, for us! We want it personal.

Where there is disagreement over these ideas of birth control is not in the areas of naturalness or artificiality or in the real need for responsible sizing of a family. The disagreement is over the real relationship between intercourse, which can happen frequently, and conception, which happens more rarely in comparison. The question is, "Is it only a remote statistical relationship or really a closer causal one?" In other words, *does every act of intercourse have to intend to be open to the possibility of life?* Because most acts of intercourse do not lead to conception, does that mean they are not as strongly causally related to each other? If not, then intercourse could have its own purpose that is less related to conception, such as the mutual good and happiness of the partners. If intercourse is not always connected to new life, then foreplay such as oral sex, would also have its own purpose, which could be the giving and receiving of love between married partners. If intercourse is causally related, then it cannot be separated from the intention to be open to the possibility of life. The church has consistently and strongly taught for many years that it is— but not infallibly.

Many good and holy people are on both sides of this issue, but unfortunately the debate is rarely civil in the media or public discourse. Even so, the answer can never really be discerned at the level of mere voting or opinion polling anyway or even public demonstrations. Like all moral issues, it can only be discerned from the viewpoint of God, Who designed the whole thing in the first place. We need to discover and believe *what He intended.* Only He can say what is ultimately good or not. The church can only reveal the will of God. The church cannot teach new doctrines on its own but must be obedient to the faith *as it has been received.* Jesus promised over and over again that He would be with us until the end of time and in that guiding presence is the wisdom we need. Discerning this issue means looking to the Lord for the answer, as the church does in prayer, scriptures, and tradition. The church can only profess what has always been believed and taught and handed down from Jesus.

Abortion

Our faith always sees at least two people in every situation involving abortion. There is always a mother, and there is always a child. Of course, others are usually involved as well, such as the father and other relatives, but at the very core of the issue are the lives of two people—mother and child. Both are persons and have all the Garden qualities common to us all. Both are free, equal, good, and helpmates to each other. Both have received the gift of life, which comes from God. Nothing can ever block or deny those Garden qualities or take that gift away for any reason. After all, they are God-given, and if He does not take them away, we cannot!

However, these two lives are intimately entwined in a way that is not paralleled in any other human experience. In what way are they separate, and in what way are they together? This issue involves very intricate and difficult-to-define balance points between mother, child, and society. We believe there are three balance points in abortion. One balances the needs of the mother with the needs of the child. The second is a secular, legal balance and compares the political *freedom* of the mother with the *life* of the child. The third one balances the needs of this new family with society.

All moral questions about abortion must include
acknowledging that at least two people are involved.

Both are human lives, both are sacred, both are in the image of God, and both are part of our human community in the Garden. They are in balance. One is not more loved by God than the other. The first balance cannot place one person over the other even though there is such an obvious developmental difference. Life is life, whether it is very young or very old, beautiful or ugly, gifted or slow, wealthy or poor, well or sick, tall or short, born or unborn. The dignity of ourselves is not based on our own talents, personalities, or attractive attributes. It comes from simply being human, a person created by God.

The second balance is political and legal and compares the two values of life and liberty. In our political understanding, as developed most famously in the Declaration of Independence, they are given equal weight ("Life, Liberty, and the Pursuit of Happiness"). That has caused much political and legal debate, for there are some cases that ask for a preference, especially between life and freedom (or choice).

Our Catholic religious tradition places *innocent* life on a slightly higher level. Innocent life is seen as a higher value than liberty. This means we cannot freely choose to take *someone else's* life, although we can freely choose to give *our own* away in love. This is part of our God-given human nature and reveals why some people will run into a fire to save someone else or jump into a river and rescue a drowning person. Innocent human life in trouble brings out instinctively, spontaneously, and naturally the most amazing heroic feats in us.

Others place liberty, or the ability to choose, on a higher level than innocent life and will allow precedence to the moral choice of one person to end another's life when that life is unborn. Sometimes the motive is compelling, as when the mother's life is at stake or the child is the result of rape or incest. Sometimes the reason is simple convenience. In all cases, the choice ends a life. *Choice* and *life* frame the political and legal debate. Each side has a considerable number of thoughtful, good, and faithful people arguing the case, as well as intolerant and uncharitable people. As Catholics, our participation in this debate must include all the respect that is due every living person, no matter what that person's position is on abortion. We present our case strongly, effectively, and with great courage but also with respect, love, and patience for those who disagree. We can act no differently than Our Lord did in similar circumstances (Mark 10:21; Matt 9:12).

Society must also balance its needs with this new family of mother and child. For example, a child conceived as a result of a crime, such as incest or rape, is not "in on" or does not participate in the circumstances of its own conception and so is still innocent. But the rest of the community must not be uncaring of its hurting members as were Adam, Eve, and Cain. All of us, our own Garden community, must feel harmony and concern with this vulnerable family. Mother and child deserve much protection, much support, and much care. Respect for new life includes the entire family into which a new person has just been conceived, even if that new life is the result of a crime. A living person is still a living person, whether old or young, poor or rich, innocent or guilty, unaware of its origin in crime or the very one responsible for it.

Choice and *life* are the two highly charged words used today to frame this sensitive moral and political debate. We believe we are not morally free to choose against innocent life, whether it is the mother or the child, whether it is legal or not. We must affirm both mother and child in love and protection. We are not choosing well when we choose behavior that is against our own nature of being helpmates to others, especially the weak, especially a mother and a child. We must do all we can for both, for they are connected in the most intimate and personal way and will remain so no matter what choice is made.

So far we have discussed issues with which people have struggled throughout history. Today we have new issues not faced in biblical times. The speed of modern technology to change our world also brings forward moral issues our ancestors never faced. We will look at several of these now.

In Vitro Birth Methods

Some couples have physical problems that prevent normal conception or childbirth and yet deeply desire a family. Do these parents have a right to have children? Does it matter how? Does desire for children have any limits? Recently, that desire has inspired modern medicine to discover amazing new ways of conceiving outside the womb, using laboratory vessels and other medical procedures. This is a very fast changing technology that bypasses the normal conception process by taking a woman's egg and a man's sperm and joining them in a laboratory dish or other venue for conception. After a successful conception, which we deeply believe is the very beginning of an innocent human life, the nascent human cells are then returned to a woman's womb to continue normal development. That new birth brings great joy to the new parents. So what are the moral balance points in all of this? Do parents have a right to have children and to have them in any way possible?

If life is a gift from God, then everything we need for wisdom in this case is in that very idea of a *"gift."* While there is a right to life once conceived, there is no prior "right to be conceived." After all, a gift cannot be demanded. It is God's autonomous free act and not a response to our will. Our attitude toward children changes because of that very graciousness of God. We see children differently when they are seen as gifts and not as manufactured beings that are "made to order."

There are side issues that muddy the moral waters as well because there are several types of "in vitro" methods. They differ on whether the egg and the sperm donors are married to each other or not, as well as the relationship of the donor wombperson, or surrogate mother, to the family. The legal issues can also become quite complicated when other nonfamily members are involved, whether they are contributing eggs, sperm, or wombs to the process. Of course, even the doctors are liable when the couple is not satisfied with the results. After all, they are paying for a successful birth. What if the child has a later-discovered learning disability or disease? Who is at fault? Is anyone really at fault? It becomes difficult to determine who is liable for what unwanted attributes of a child. Is it the doctors? The donors? God?

We believe that once conceived, a child has a right to life that is stable, nourishing for growth, and loving. Of course, no one ever gets it all perfectly, but at least we shouldn't intend directly against it. How we start our life is important and contributes to our sense of personal dignity and self-worth. We have already seen the role of sex as a centerpiece of marital love. Passionate lovemaking is a core experience of marriage and the origin of life. It makes sense that children would know that they were created from that real act of passionate love of their own parents and that they were naturally endowed with a mixture of traits from each.

Of course, we rejoice at every life, no matter how it is begun. Every life is cherished. Although everyone feels deeply for the childless couple, *how* they go about obtaining a child is important. For example, they just can't kidnap or purchase a child. Legal methods, such as adoption, certainly help a child as well as the family. We believe in vitro methods just tip the balance away from the natural human dignity that comes from conception as a direct consequence of the actions of parental lovemaking. However, these medical methods do not invalidate that new life, for every life is precious.

At present though, this procedure has a high failure rate of conception. It must be tried several times, and each time must include *several egg-sperm conceptions* in one dish. Not just one egg can be reliably used. The statistical odds increase when doctors include more conception possibilities, especially in this still fairly new medical procedure. Even though several conceptions occur, usually only one is taken for a mother's womb development. The others are destroyed or stored. Because we consider each conception a brand new life, that destruction forces our will unfairly on an innocent person. It is an act of abortion. We have unfairly made a life-or-death decision for the other embryos.

There are some methods that show promise. They are medically complex and have subtle ethical concerns. The

1987 church letter *Donum Vitae* ("Gift of Life") has a more detailed description of them. One procedure extracts the egg and sperm medically and then allows them to join in the mother's body naturally for continued gestation. Science continues to explore new options, as it should, for our intellect is also a gift from God and we should use it to the maximum of our ability. We need to use our wisdom to the maximum, as well as keep all our actions moral. It makes for a healthier life!

Genetic Engineering and Cloning

Genes are complex molecules in our DNA that guide the process of human development. During the earliest stages of cell development scientists can manipulate the genetic makeup of a new person and so change how a person grows. Why do this? Some speculate that there are individual genes for such specific human traits as intelligence, athletic ability, or even diseases like cancer. If identified, these genes could be manipulated to "craft" people with or without those traits. Naturally, some fear that unscrupulous or bigoted people or even totalitarian governments might create a "master race." For example, they could produce "people to order" by manufacturing only short muscular blondes or tall smart redheads or even by preventing unwanted disabled people from arriving at all. What is the morality of these techno-births?

This is such a brand new area that is moving so fast that it is hard to think about it morally. If our motive is to alter people genetically for *our own needs,* that is clearly wrong.

People are not possessions. Our motive must be only to help. Yet sometimes it is not easy to distinguish good and bad motives. If the desire is genuinely to help a person medically by removing a physical problem, say, a genetic predisposition to cancer, we might be tempted to support it. We should certainly work to protect ourselves from disease and whatever might be a predisposition for it. However, this field is still so new we don't know what may be the unintended consequences. For example, protecting against one disease may make us vulnerable to new ones. But what if the temptation is to achieve some kind of physical "perfection" or to "correct" some problem? That can mean many different things. Just what needs perfection? What is a "problem?" Is it shortness? Baldness? Left-handedness? Low IQ? Who decides?

The Human Genome Project is a massive scientific enterprise of both government and private laboratories that seeks to understand the sequence and role of genes in our DNA code. Recent discoveries indicate we have a much smaller number of genes than first thought. Each gene may guide our predisposition to several traits or features or even make sure certain traits never appear. How they are turned on or off may be a combination of many factors that are not yet fully understood. Most likely, we are who we are by a combination of nature *and* nurture, of genetic programming *and* environmental factors, of DNA *and* the quality of our family, friendships, schooling, and career. For example, the exact genetic replica of a professional golfer such as Tiger Woods may grow up to be a violin player, a teacher, or a librarian instead. Genetic engineering is not the easy answer to mass-producing desired human personalities.

Of course, we want to remove pain from the lives of our loved ones. No doubt about that. Yet pain, disappointment, disabilities, obstacles, and hardships are also some of the most formative experiences of life. While no one should seek suffering, it is in *meeting* these events head-on that we really grow and reveal our humanity. There will always be some form of suffering to face, and how we face it both reveals and forms us. The soft and easy life is really no life at all. We remain children when never challenged. We are at our best when we play the genetic hand we were dealt with courage, creativity, and grace.

Genetic engineering is the area of moral discourse that will be very important in the near future. It will be a stimulating and productive debate, for it will cause us to relook at what are the best and worst events of human experience. We will need to pray more and seek the wisdom of God to reflect on the place of suffering in our life and the moral ways to remove it.

Cloning is a specific type of genetic engineering that is very new. There are two main types of cloning methods today: Embryonic Twinning and Adult DNA Cloning. Embryonic Twinning is a way to copy the natural process of making twins and uses a normal, fertilized egg. Although we have many different cells in our body, like liver cells, brain cells, and skin cells, almost every cell contains the entire genetic blueprint for a whole human being. *Every* cell could theoretically be *any* cell in the body. However, soon after the first few cell divisions after conception, our DNA code determines that only certain genes in each cell will activate at certain times, which then enables cells to differentiate into their many types, such as skin, liver, and muscle cells. In Embryonic Twinning, a cell is divided and separated before DNA differentiation starts, and each is allowed to replicate. The DNA differentiation process then begins in the separated cell, and they will grow into separate persons who are genetically identical to each other, that is, as twins. In the Adult DNA Cloning Method, recent progress has been made in "reprogramming" *adult* cells of certain animals, such as sheep, to behave as they were before they were differentiated by DNA activation. It is not clear if this process can happen with adult human cells yet.

Cloning means there is no joining of genetic material from two parents. The child is a genetic replica, not a descendent. However, genetic mixing was important in our evolutionary development as humans. It enhanced the evolutionary success of our species. It continues to protect us from potential abnormalities. We are who we are today by this God-given system of regeneration. No one can know yet how a change in genetic programming will affect our future. We have already seen in the section on genetic engineering that simply cloning a famous person like Tiger Woods may not likely result in a new person with the same golf skills. Even so, we believe the cloned person does have a soul and so is worthy of the same dignity as all people. However, as always, we also believe people have the right to be born of love and to know their origin as arising from an act of passionate love between two people. One blessing of the "lottery" system of genetic mixing is the acceptance each person receives from loving parents as he or she arrives in the world naturally. Persons are not seen as products but as wonderful surprises. Cloning "crafts people to order" for sometimes selfish reasons. There is a great moral difference between loving children for who they are and crafting them to be who we want.

Homosexuality

There are three common claims made about homosexual orientation: (a) It is a genetic or inherited condition and so is a natural part of some people's makeup. (b) It is an unconscious choice caused by hidden psychological forces. (c) It is a conscious choice made in personal freedom. Our faith actually makes no stand on any of these issues about cause or origin. That is more a question for psychology and medicine. However, because sexual intercourse includes openness to the possibility of new life, it does not make sense for a homosexual couple to engage in that intercourse that connotes openness to life. Although a lot of other good qualities may be present in their relationship, we must acknowledge what is not present, as well. However, a deep love between any two same-sex persons may include other physical expressions of their relationship that are less intimate than intercourse. The section on sexual love describes in more detail our understanding of the importance of physical intimacy in all relationships.

It is also important to remember that not all same-sex affection is homosexual. Different cultures have their own customs for same-sex behavior. For example, stereotypically, some Mediterranean countries are much more demonstrative in showing affection than, say, northern European cultures. However, no matter what the culture or ethnic background or even orientation, all relationships between persons require respect for all the Garden virtues. The freedom of partners, their goodness, equality, and need to love must always guide behavior.

Orientation and behavior are two ideas often confused in understanding homosexuality. The first may be inherited, but the latter is chosen. For example, some people may have inherited traits or genetic inclinations to a physical problem such as cancer or alcohol, whereas others may have a predisposition for personality issues such as depression or even violence. Any one of those predispositions can greatly influence a person's life. But an inherited trait cannot excuse any reckless, irresponsible, or violent acts by any person. Although it might help in understanding the person and his or her motives, it does not condone anything. Our actions are fully our responsibility. Although it is true that every person is "given" a set of genetic circumstances at birth, such as inherited talent, race, health, and certain personality attributes, they are not *deterministic* of behavior. We are not robots unable to choose freely. Although at times more difficult for some, our freedom is the very basis for saying we are responsible human beings.

The Christian challenge is to live the way of Jesus *no matter what our circumstances are,* to follow Jesus *in spite* of circumstances. We can never allow any part of life to become an excuse for mistreating or hurting another. Of course, at no time does homosexual orientation or behavior excuse or justify discrimination from anyone. No matter how it is lived, every human life is worthy of respect and dignity.

Discussion Starters

1. What are some of the common mistakes people make in finding a marriage partner?

2. Infatuation, crush, codependent, and lust, are some names of relationships. Make a list of as many as you can, and describe each of them with examples.

3. What would be three qualities that help marriages to be happy and lasting? What would be three qualities that endanger marriages?

4. Describe the most loving relationship you have had or now have.

5. What is your idea of the right role of sexual behavior between friends, lovers, engaged couples, and married couples?

6. Discuss your ideas about whether every act of sexual intercourse should be open to the possibility of life.

7. What are your feelings about the scientific progress being made today in genetic engineering?

8. Describe the family rules in your home when you were a child. What would be your choices for five healthy family rules?

9. How would you counsel a childless couple that desperately wanted to have a child?

10. How do you feel about someone who holds the opposite opinion of yours about abortion?

CHAPTER 4

Social Issues

Alcoholism and Substance Abuse

Alcohol and all other mood-altering drugs accomplish the same goal. They change the way we feel quickly. They are almost always guaranteed to provide a sense of euphoria and good feelings for a relatively short period of time. That is their attraction. They change the chemistry of the brain to produce these effects. A depressed person can artificially change his or her mood quickly and assuredly with drugs. They are "self-prescribed" medications to ease the pain of living. Some drugs, such as alcohol, can be used in moderation. Others, such as cocaine, can be deadly at any level. With improper use they all have horrific additional physical, psychological, and spiritual effects. In various ways, drugs and alcohol cause great damage to internal organs, such as the liver, the lungs, the heart, and especially brain tissues. This kind of self-inflicted wound could never be the plan of God for creatures he created already good. Relying on chemical "crutches" to provide a chemically induced mood is not genuine. It is not the truth of our personality, and only the truth will set us free (John 8:32).

Drug abuse keeps people living excessively on a feeling level. Because of their assured and quick effects, drugs can cause a dependency on these euphoric feelings and intolerance for any of life's challenges or hardships. Instead of facing issues with the virtues of courage, fidelity, hard work, and faith, people will rely on these chemicals to induce a general numbness to the world. However, it is the challenge in life that causes growth. Avoiding them with chemicals returns us to an infantile childlike state. Hardly the plan of God for us.

Some chemicals, such as most narcotics and nicotine, produce an actual physiological dependency or addiction, others capitalize on individual genetic and hereditary predispositions, as does alcohol. Those predispositions can predict who may have the potential for drug trouble but can never be an excuse for it. Whether the dependency results from heredity, physical adaptation, or psychological weakness, none of them removes personal responsibility for using drugs. For example, some people do have a genetic and familial history that might predispose them for violence, but that cannot excuse violent behavior. In the same way, the disease of alcoholism may certainly be a factor in diagnosis and especially in treatment but can never be an excuse for behavior.

Addictive behaviors are, by definition, selfish. An addicted person thinks only of the drug that will alter mood. That need becomes paramount and tragically takes over all other needs, including those of family and friends. An addicted person may be willing to sacrifice anything—a good career, a home, family savings, in order to secure the desired feeling of euphoria, even if only for a few hours at a time. Other people, even loved ones, may have significance to the addict only to the extent that they can provide, hide, or enhance the use of the drug. It is a very serious problem and usually very difficult to change. Any behavior that allows, tolerates, or encourages the use of drugs in others is just as immoral. Codependent behavior can also be an addiction and just as selfish as drug abuse. Both people are meeting powerful selfish needs—one needs drugs, whereas the other may have a psychological addiction to being needed or being seen as a martyr and a victim.

Most dangerous drugs are highly illegal. Their use adds the moral problem of criminal activity. However, some of the most dangerous and deadly drugs are perfectly legal, such as nicotine and alcohol. Because of their social acceptance—indeed, almost required presence at social gatherings—their abuse can easily be masked. The addiction can be hidden under social party-going behavior. These drugs enjoy general societal approval, even when used excessively. Worse still, as a legal business, their manufacturers can lawfully promote them with ad campaigns that associate their use with other desired qualities, such as success, money, and sophistication. The easy accessibility of these drugs demands, even more, that our head be in charge of behavior and not our heart.

Alcoholics Anonymous (AA) is the most successful program so far for the treatment of addictions. While not for everyone, it has an excellent track record of success for many people. It is a program based on twelve steps and group gatherings in which addicts confront, counsel, and talk with each other. The twelve steps affirm, among other ideas, the right relationship between God's power and our abilities: our responsibility to choose wisely, our responsibility for our behavior to others, and our inherent goodness. They are a wonderful summary of the Garden virtues of equality, goodness, freedom, and service to others.

Sometimes a family will resort to an "intervention" to help an addict. Family, friends, and coworkers of the addict will "intervene" or confront the addict as a group and convince him or her to enter a treatment program. Addiction is so strong that sometimes dramatic action is necessary. If the intervention is done with love and authenticity, it can work very well. An intervention dramatically reconnects an addict to a sense of responsibility to others and self. It can break the cycle of addictive selfishness. However, if it is meant to overpower or force the addict to comply, it usually does not last. No treatment program that offends Garden virtues can really be therapeutic. A deep experience of our freedom, goodness, and equality and a desire to help others is the ultimate mood-altering event.

Child Abuse

This is an especially serious form of violence. Treating a young person as an object to be used for personal gratification violates every one of the Garden virtues. Child abuse removes freedom, denies equality, denigrates the innate goodness of children who are loved by God, and in no way helps them. This abuse seriously wounds other people, especially at an age when the children have few emotional and intellectual resources to defend themselves against it, much less recover afterward.

There are various forms of this violence. Some involve physical violence alone and include excessive corporal punishment. Some are acts of emotional violence and include excessive criticism, neglect, and abandonment. Some are sexual behaviors and include everything from fondling to full sexual contact. All involve one person exercising his or her will over and against another. All involve profound levels of selfishness by the perpetrator.

All are serious, but each may have different lasting consequences for the victim. While it is certain the perpetrator has a severe psychological problem, we cannot automatically know what the impact will be for the victim. After all, the child might be very young, so it becomes difficult to assess the level of psychological trauma. It all depends on what the meaning of the experience was for him or her. The trauma for the victim depends on several factors: age, maturity, relationship to perpetrator, frequency of the events, duration of the experience, and intensity of the acts. All these factors combine to give a good picture of the severity of the trauma. However, no matter how terrible the experience, it is a firm bedrock of our faith that we are able to recover from any and all experiences. Professional counselors, spiritual directors, friends, family, and medical doctors, are all resources that can combine to chart a road back to health. At some point, the child must come to hear the voice of God within his or her heart that reaffirms innate goodness and human dignity, equality with all peoples, freedom to be him or herself, and God's deep desire to help the child move forward. Even though some violent people may hurt or wound even the littlest members of our community, it is His will that these little ones enjoy life to the fullest and that their joy may be complete (John 10:10).

Euthanasia

Sometimes suffering is so unbearable that sick people just want to die. These are such tragic times for the person and also the family and friends who painfully watch such suffering in their loved one. Some are tempted to help actively in assisting their suicide. That act has a Greek word to describe it, *euthanasia* (*eu* = good + *thanos* = death).

Here, the mystery of suffering has a most compelling impact. What was the response of Jesus when faced with His own cross? In the Garden of Gethsemane, He asked to be spared the cross but would, nevertheless, face it with courage and faith. We are faced with the mystery of a God who did not spare His own Son (Rom 8:32). We stand in awe at the majesty of Jesus who faced His passion with peace and courage. But like Jesus, we don't have to seek it or look for it. If it comes our way, we try to face it with the same courage and peace as He did. We will need Him with us to do so.

Fortunately, modern medicine has extremely effective pain-relieving procedures in use today. There is almost no reason for patients to be in chronic pain. Using ordinary means to avoid pain is certainly moral, such as these painkilling medicines and the latest scientific procedures. Using ordinary means to avoid or delay death is also moral, such as preventative health measures. But using extraordinary means to prolong suffering, or even life itself, is not necessary. Jesus didn't, so we don't. Removing life support or refusing emergency resuscitation for those with a *fatal and certain diagnosis* preserves the dignity of natural death. God still determines the moment of death.

Of course, "extraordinary" changes with time. What was extraordinary in 1940 is ordinary today. However, directly intending to kill someone cannot ever be moral. If life is a gift, then God does not give gifts to be refused. The reason that killing anyone is wrong is that we are not in charge of the basic existence of people. That was what Adam and Eve forgot. If I cannot decide to end *your* life, I cannot do it for *myself* either. Euthanasia takes that power away from God. Not a good thing to do! It is one thing to remove life support and let an inevitable natural death occur for a sick friend; it is another to make death happen or to assist in people killing themselves.

Capital Punishment

The fifth commandment is "Thou shalt not kill." However, our tradition teaches that this "killing" means taking *innocent* life, so capital punishment is not murder. After all, we have a responsibility to care for the life God gave us and the lives of others who are in our care, such as a child by a parent or citizens by their leader. The state may use force to stop unjust aggressors or even to put them to death if there is *no other means* available. Generally, it should use the least amount of violence possible. The killing of another in self-defense is not a murder by the state or a citizen if there was simply no other way to stop the aggressor from killing again. This idea has a long history in our tradition. However, modern states have many new tools, such as high-tech prisons and better laws, to protect society from criminals ever killing again. How can a modern state be defenseless today? The circumstances allowing capital punishment are just too rare.

Still, even though capital punishment is morally possible, our motive can make a difference. For example, some motives that drive the use of the death penalty today are punishment, deterrence, and revenge. Punishment is any kind of legal sentence that is painful or uncomfortable. Of course, it must be proportionate to the crime and for the purpose of *helping* the offender *change* behavior and repent. When the offender authentically accepts the sentence, it can lead to great personal change. Pain is a powerful motivator. It rivets our attention. It triggers intense emotions and so makes anything learned more enduring. However, we cannot punish just for the purpose of inflicting pain. Revenge can never be a moral reason for punishment. It places society at the same level as the criminal, and it can even increase violence. For example, an executed criminal may have family members who might now feel the need to take revenge themselves for the death of their relative. Violence creates violence, and revenge stops repentance.

Obviously, an executed criminal cannot repent, but the execution might cause others to change. That is the "deterrence" argument. But it is almost impossible to know if deterrence works. Criminal behavior is psychologically complex, which makes it difficult to find causes. Moreover, cities with high or low crime rates do not correlate well with cities with or without capital punishment sufficiently to draw clear conclusions. Of course, facing death is compelling to anyone who thinks rationally about the consequences of his or her behavior. But usually crime is precisely an *irresponsible* behavior arising from *not* thinking clearly about consequences. Most likely, it is the *certainty* of punishment and not the *severity* that deters more effectively. We cannot take a human life with only a vague statistical hope it will stop others from crime. Capital punishment is only allowed, and then reluctantly, when there is absolutely no other possible way of defending against further crime by the violent person.

Social Justice

Justice is giving someone what is his or her due. In the Garden of Eden, God made us free, equal, good, and helpmates to one another. That means we not only enjoy these gifts ourselves but owe them to everyone else as well. In fact, God precisely created us to be socially oriented to others. So our answer to Cain's question, "Am I my brother's keeper?" is a resounding, "Yes!" The welfare of others *is* our concern precisely because we were made in the image of God. Therefore, social justice is a natural part of our makeup, not a choice only for those so inclined. Moreover, we believe God so *loved* the world that He sent His only Son to be our Savior (John 3:16). If God feels that strongly about His creatures, well, we must also. In fact, where we stand with God is the measure of where we stand with each other, especially those most in need (Matt 25). Christians act justly when they care for anyone in need but especially those at the margins of society: the most vulnerable, the sick, the elderly, the young, the prisoners, and those oppressed by aggression. Jesus made Himself one of these least ones so that we might notice them also. Salvation is for all people so the Gospel is always "social justice" in that it is about that salvation and the peace, justice, and human dignity that God has promised us all.

But how does that work practically, especially when a poor, homeless person walks up to you on the street and asks for a handout? What is the moral thing to do? What if the person is mentally ill or wants money for alcohol or looks as if he or she might be violent? There are several moral options. Some people might give money right away and hope the person will use it responsibly. Others will become more involved and personally take the person to a restaurant or store to get needed supplies. Others will refuse immediate aid but contribute generously to social agencies that provide more comprehensive and perhaps more enduring help. Still others might work in politics to change the economic conditions that contribute to homelessness or poverty. All of the above show some care for the homeless person. They range from the most immediate actions to more systemic efforts. *What is unacceptable is to do nothing.* Whether we support agencies or get involved personally in giving aid or give money away in direct street encounters, we must do something. God made us our brother and sister's keeper. What we cannot do in the face of human suffering is nothing.

Some issues, such as poverty, or welfare, or homelessness are just too big for one person to affect. They have a larger context and so are called "social sins." They involve injustices in large structures like the world economy or the way a particular nation or company does business. But just as one person did not set up capitalism, communism, socialism, or multinational companies, it cannot be one person who can change them. Moral behavior sometimes involves many people working together for many years to accomplish goals that might seem impossible to reach at first. Each person might work in only one area that may seem remote from the goal, but it is important work, and it has a dignity that is important. If there is anything in the practical application of sinful social structures that infringes on the dignity of the human person, like a company exploiting workers or a government polluting the environment, it must be changed. But it will be long, slow work. It is tempting to take a shortcut.

Can a person break the law to achieve some good moral aim? That kind of action is called civil disobedience, and its morality requires a high level of honest judgment and serious reflection. Obviously, we don't believe that ends justify means, but can moral behavior sometimes require this kind of dramatic, illegal action? For example, some of the marches in the Civil Rights movement in the 1960s broke local codes on lawful assembly or trespassing ordinances. Yet, there is nothing inherently wrong with marching, and certainly the proportionate good achieved was much greater than the laws broken. Most importantly, breaking the law was not the *principle* intention of the marchers. It was an unintended side effect. Still, sometimes an unjust law is broken deliberately but for the main purpose of initiating a constitutional challenge to it, as in the case of legal challenges to codified racial discrimination. A law must be broken in order to achieve judicial review. Honest and serious reflection can help ensure that our intentions and actions are moral and not misguided or based mostly upon adolescent difficulties with authority. Motives, actions, and circumstances all must have an inherent goodness to them, even if serious side effects result. Moral decision making will often cause conflict and struggle between groups on different sides of issues. It takes courage and strength to become involved.

Nevertheless, despite the challenges, Catholics for centuries have built schools to educate young people, hospitals to heal the sick, and social agencies to help the poor. They have also lobbied governments for societal change. There is just no area of human life outside Christian concern. If people are involved, then so is the church. That is why periodically the church will speak out on seemingly "secular" issues, such as politics, the economy, or business. These are areas of intense human endeavor. They each influence the quality of our lives directly and powerfully. Therefore, they are Christian issues. For example, are people able to work at decent and safe jobs? Do citizens have a say in their political affairs? Are political leaders accountable to their citizens? Do the courts operate justly? Do the commercial markets operate fairly? Does a company treat its employees with dignity?

Is the tax system fair? Does this new technology enhance or degrade our dignity as persons? A political system, an economic enterprise, or a technological innovation is moral when it either enhances or is, at least, neutral toward our Garden virtues. In each new area, we bring a desire to ensure peace, justice, and human dignity. We try to live the moral behavior that is the sign and safeguard of those values.

Violence and Revenge

Violence is the use of physical or emotional force against another person and against that person's will. Violence is serious business and has a long and tragic history in human affairs. It causes immense damage to both victims *and* perpetrators, and the consequences can last for years. Ironically, the very fear of violence can drive our desire for learning moral behavior precisely because it is so dangerous and catastrophic to human life. We need to understand and control this problem. One day perhaps, with our prayers and hard work, it will disappear.

Violence offends against every Garden virtue. It violates the freedom, goodness, helpmateness, and equality of a person who is our brother or sister in the Lord. For example, violent people see others not as persons but as things, objects, or obstacles and use force to subdue, remove, or eliminate them. Violence may be impulsive, as in a barroom brawl, or planned, as in a premeditated crime. It may be personal, as in spousal abuse, or institutional, as in armed combat and warfare. In all cases, violent people aggressively *impose* their will on others.

One source of violence is revenge. Violent people may actually justify their actions by recalling a past hurt done to them by the victim, and revenge is their retaliation or reprisal for that perceived hurt. It is a powerful motive and strong enough to counter our very nature as helpmates to one another. It began early in our history.

The very next story in the Bible after Adam and Eve is the story of revenge and violence. Two brothers, Cain and Abel, present gifts to God, but Cain is angry that his gift is rejected. He mistakenly feels his relationship with God is threatened. He knows that relationship is the source of his human dignity and self-esteem, so he is devastated by this perceived loss of status.

Cain blames Abel. He is jealous of Abel's approval by God and is jealous of Abel's good fortune. He sees Abel as a competitor for a perceived finite amount of God's favor. Wanting what another person has, or competing for what is perceived as scarce goods are common preconditions to attacking another. When Abel receives what Cain wants, Cain feels threatened, belittled, and dismissed. He wants revenge.

Any attack on our personal dignity strikes some of the deepest parts of our personality and may cause powerful emotions. In human evolution, as well as in each child's development, the part of our brain that feels emotions develops first, before higher cognitive areas are formed. The most primitive and basic threats to our existence, such as a threat against dignity or physical safety, are emotionally registered there first and are not easily modulated later by higher reasoning, logic, or even common sense. These emotional reactions are primordial and may seem exaggerated or overblown. That's because they are triggered by events that are *emotionally perceived* as life threatening and so may include such intense feelings.

These emotional wounds are difficult to heal. For example, if I steal a dollar from your wallet, it is easy to repair that "monetary" wound. I simply replace the dollar in your wallet. However, if I injure your feelings, I cannot simply replace them like I can a dollar bill. It will take time for you to heal. Hurt feelings are emotional wounds and require much more than simply returning money. Our personal sense of self comprises a complex constellation of psychic events that includes a lot of emotions. That is why feelings are so closely connected to our sense of our selves as persons, to our dignity and self-respect, and to our self-esteem. If I injure your dignity, I may arouse an emotional firestorm. In the Genesis story, Cain is hurt and angry and that leads to an unfortunate but predictable chain of events.

For example, perhaps you can remember when another person hurt you. That wound can cause the strong reaction that from the beginning of human history has been a cause of so much human misery. It is the impulse for revenge, and it is a common cause of violence. Revenge seeks reprisal. *It wants the other person to feel the same experience that we felt when we were wounded.* We want to "get back" at them. We want to "get even," or "to balance the books," and so we strike back in an attempt to do so. However, we must remember that emotions are driving our behavior, so our actions may be a little wild. What usually happens is some form of inaccuracy in our "aim." Our attack is either too weak or too strong. If too weak, we attack again and again, still looking for satisfaction but usually going too far, now causing our opponent to feel unjustly hurt. He or she then feels the impulse for retaliation and attacks back and continues to attack, until the attack goes too far, causing another impulse for revenge by you. This cycle of revenge continues back and forth, but—and this is the crucial point—*it always escalates*. It is impossible simply to "get even." The cycle of revenge will escalate to murderous violence until something stops it. In the Genesis story, Cain killed Abel.

Sometimes revenge is stopped by social convention or even death. For example, if you are angry with your boss at work, you may be unable to get revenge because you will be fired. Maybe your "enemy" is now a deceased relative. In either case, the vengeful impulse remains within you in an arrested state called "resentment," or "frozen revenge." The attitude and the desire for violence remain, although not expressed outwardly. It stays as ruminations or evil thoughts or is expressed as passive-aggressive behavior in which attacks are made in a way that hides the source.

Hiding, denial, and regression are common excuses used to explain away violence: "I don't know what came over me." "I was caught up in the crowd that did this!" "You made me do this!" Because violence is so opposite of our nature, is so destructive of all that we value in human life, and runs counter to common sense, people may actually hide, deny, or repress its presence, its causes, or its consequences. Ironically, violent people often hide or deny their behavior because they think it offensive to see themselves as violent!

Blame and deflection are also common excuses. Adam tries hiding in the Garden after the Fall. Cain at first denies and then deflects God's inquiry by asking God the question, "Am I my brother's keeper?" The people ready to stone the woman caught in adultery in John 8:3 are hiding within a mob. When a mob finds a target, people regress to childlike behavior and give over their will to the group and the group leader to mask their own responsibility for violent action. Jesus confronts the mob and returns individuals to responsibility by inviting *each one* to think of his or her past actions. "Let the one without sin cast the first stone." Ironically, sin unites the crowd with the woman. They cannot "demonize" one who is the same as themselves. They cannot stone one of their own. In addition, the first stone tossed would have given an excuse for the rest to "go along with the crowd" and stone her to death. Jesus stops the first stone by demanding that people take responsibility and not hide in the mob. Jesus knows how to deal with us!

Revenge is powerful enough to counter our God-given nature to see other persons as free, equal, and good helpmates. The level of a victim's personal trauma and damage is strongly affected by three factors: (1) how frequently he or she was hurt; (2) how intense the violence was; and (3) how long it lasted. Frequency, intensity, and duration are factors that indicate the severity of the wound and the strength of revenge impulse. At all levels, violence and revenge are corrosive. They eat away at the virtues present in all of us. Yet what is to be done? How does a person handle the myriad hurts and offenses that come during the day? How are we to "turn the other cheek?" What kind of person can turn the other cheek? Are we meant to be doormats? What is the Lord asking of us?

Two brief stories reveal something of the Lord's wisdom: Several people worked together at a job at which there was suddenly great anxiety. A new owner was arriving soon, and there would be some layoffs. Everyone took out his or her frustration on the youngest and most recently hired person. The employees gossiped, lied, insulted, tricked, and hurt the person in many ways. Yet throughout it all, the person was calm and peaceful. He never sought revenge. When asked if he was upset at such harassment, he replied, "Not really; you see, I'm the son of the new owner!" Well, when you have a special relationship with the boss, it doesn't matter what the others do to you; your job is secure. When we have a strong relationship with God, it doesn't matter what others do to us. We know we are loved and treasured by the God of the universe. Only God can tell us who we are, and He thinks we are wonderful!

In another example, an elementary school teacher with an abusive spouse hears offensive insults all day long at home, yet *doesn't* take personally the insults of a young student at school because the child is clearly an immature and ignorant child. Well, so is *anyone* who insults us. If the child really knew the value of the teacher, he or she wouldn't do it, neither

would any adult. While dying, Jesus looked at His execu-
tioners and said, "Father, forgive them; they know not what
they are doing (they are all ignorant children)." With this
idea, we can turn the other cheek only because the first slap
was *not experienced as a wound*. There is no need to seek
revenge. That brings a wonderful side benefit. Avoiding the
revenge cycle frees us to discern calmly in the criticism of
others any kernel of truth that *might be* embedded in their
attack and from which we can learn and change for the better. We are free to experience calmly and judge objectively
the hurtful actions of others to ourselves. We stay the master
of our reactions to the world around us. We remain at peace.

Forgiveness and Healing

Of course, if you are deeply hurt, there is the danger of
the escalating cycle of revenge. You might feel that need to
"get back and get even," or if revenge is not possible, you feel
that resentment, or "frozen revenge." However, we know it is
impossible to "get even," and so you might consider forgiveness even in the midst of pain. Forgiveness is a *decision to not
seek revenge*. It is more a decision than a feeling. You may still
feel terrible, and you are *not forgetting* what happened or
ignoring the event. You may even have to avoid this other
dangerous person completely. You may still feel the need for
some explanation of why someone hurt you, still feel a need
for his or her repentance, your healing, and mutual reconciliation. Forgiveness, however, is very different from healing,
which involves our feelings and takes more time. It may come

slowly as we receive an explanation of what happened or some reason why this hurt occurred. Healing continues when we see the other person express sorrow, repent for the action, and change for the better. Of course, that doesn't always happen. Healing can still continue as we begin to make some sense of the meaning of the event in our whole life history. We see the larger picture and get a sense of perspective and wisdom from this suffering. The passage of some time also helps because we slowly regain our self-esteem as we continue living our life and working at our job and accomplishing things. With time, we slowly realize the message of lack of worth that violence brings is, well, just plain wrong. We realize we are a capable person with dignity after all.

Violence and the Media

There is much concern today about the impact of graphic violent imagery in movies, television, videos, and video games. It is difficult to know if these images cause violent behavior, are correlational, or have no effect at all. Many studies offer conflicting conclusions. Media forms vary in their approach to violence. For example, violence in movies occurs as part of a story, whereas in violent video games it *is* the story. It is important to look at the context. How does this particular media story treat the consequences of violence? Are people rewarded? Is violence glorified or portrayed as admirable? Are violent people vilified or presented in an admiring way? Sometimes a story that presents justice against villains in the final minute of a film will have already glorified them for the first hour. Those images can be a lasting memory for young viewers.

There is a wide variation in media experience and impact as well. For example, interactive media is more compelling because it requires more physical and mental involvement than passive video watching. However, all media require a user to access them voluntarily by buying movie tickets, renting a video, or turning on a television. There are great variations in the kind of people who access them, as well. Mature, well-adjusted viewers can probably put it all in perspective, whereas immature and less well-adjusted persons might be more easily influenced. Because there is little regulation for access to these images, the potential for the wrong people watching the wrong material is very high. If there is a causal connection between media violence and social behavior, then there is a very serious moral liability on the media to accept responsibility for violent consequences. How horrible to actually teach or lead others to violence! It would also be irresponsible for a media producer to offer potentially dangerous material without offering some ideas on the regulation about who will access it.

At the least, we can probably acknowledge that over a period of time violent imagery can desensitize any person to the horror of violence. Perhaps we can use the same trauma discernment criteria of *frequency, intensity,* and *duration* in understanding its impact. If a person watches highly intense violence frequently over a long period of time, then we might safely infer that there is a higher probability for desensitization. Yet, it is precisely that God-given sense we have of the value and dignity of other people that is our safeguard against violence. If that is dulled, we are all in trouble. Violence in the media is an issue that is deserving of continuing, thorough, and rigorous research.

Martyrdom, Heroism, and Self-Defense

Martyrs and heroes face violence courageously but with important conditions. After all, we must take care of the person we are and act safely. Our life belongs to God, and so we must care for it. We cannot accept violence to ourselves lightly. We have no right to assume a "victim" role or to allow another passively to misuse their dignity as a person by doing violent acts to us. We must uphold our dignity and theirs by stopping violence whenever we can.

We can accept violence to ourselves for heroic reasons but only if done with accurate and realistic self-knowledge of our strengths and weaknesses and a reasonable expectation of success. For example, if we think our acceptance of violence to ourselves will change the violent person for the better or inspire others to achieve some noble goal, then we are practicing heroic faith. Gandhi did this in India, as did Jesus in Jerusalem. However, we are not *required* to be heroes or martyrs. We are certainly required to know ourselves, so if we know we do not have the strength to accept violence, then we must not.

Violence against others or ourselves must always be stopped. We cannot tolerate that horrible injustice to the dignity of persons. No person is an object to be used by another. However, violence must be stopped in nonviolent ways if at all possible. Of course, in self-defense, we may use force as a last resort but only for the purpose of successfully stopping the attack, not for the purpose of injuring the other. We cannot treat our attacker as an object either. We cannot fight evil with evil. What then, are we to make of war?

War and Terrorism

Warfare is institutional violence. It brings the resources of an entire society or nation against an enemy in a massive display of force and terror. Warfare often brings to violence the latest technology for causing physical and emotional destruction. It offers the unique ferocity that only nations can provide. War is the most extreme form of violence. War is hell.

Warfare is also an engine of history. It has changed and continues to change the social landscape of how and with whom we live and work. It has changed the course of nations and empires. But at its root, it is about death and destruction. Yet, no other human enterprise in all of human history has ever marshaled the efforts of so many people in a single movement and on such a grand scale. Twice in the last century, nations from all over the globe were engaged in a world war. Warfare must be tapping into something very primordial in the human spirit. Yet it still violates all the Garden virtues.

How do loving people with families and jobs and even deep faith get caught in large-scale institutional violence against people they might have never even met? Why do good people join a group intent on causing harm to strangers? Why do they follow orders that might place them in the front lines of a battle facing murderous weapons, grotesque wounds, or horrible death? How can any military leader exercise that much power over individuals?

The dynamics of warfare are psychologically powerful and create a very strong unifying force among a nation's people. They tap into our nature as helpmates and into our desire to join with others in a common great crusade. However, it is paradoxically against our fellow human beings, our very neighbors on this planet. Among these dynamics are two aberrant forces that serve to bind individuals tightly to a group even in an action against our fellow humans. They are *regression* and *scapegoating*.

Individuals who act within large crowds, like a mob, sometimes may regress to psychologically childlike behavior. They surrender their human dignity as freethinking and responsible persons to the group and the group leader (or parent figure). They will regress to infantile aggression and rage, throwing what literally resembles a tantrum. It is behavior fueled often by childish emotions such as jealousy, fear, and envy. The actions of the crowd help to hide or mask these emotions under the guise of some larger political cause. When a national leader offers the crowd primordial needs like power, wealth, or revenge for some slight at the hands of another country, the people are likely to respond with loyalty. The tighter the group loyalty is, the more it acts as a cohesive unit, which continues to help individuals *hide their responsibility* for even wanting these needs.

Scapegoating also provides extremely strong group unity. When two people begin the cycle of escalating revenge, the result can be deadly. They can change the cycle by turning together to attack an innocent third party, the scapegoat. Excuses are quickly found to attack this innocent scapegoat. The two former enemies find peace because a new common enemy unites them against the outsider. They draw a circle around themselves that excludes the enemy as "other" and unites the both of them in a uniquely powerful way. They demonize the other person with vile propaganda as justification and excuse for scapegoating.

Ironically, people will express heroically their Garden virtues within their own group but will be willing to kill the nongroup member easily. They will heroically die for the group but never for the scapegoat. The history of war recounts tales of amazing courage, initiative, innovation, and the very best of human ingenuity but at the expense of some demonized other group. The story of warfare describes the use of our best virtues to kill, destroy, damage, and devastate all that is good about human civilization.

Jesus confronts these group dynamics by calling us to responsibility for our actions and to love our enemies. He removes the veil that covers the crowd so that they can never "hide" in a mob again. He offers no excuse for "the group excuse." Instead, Jesus calls us to form a church or an assembly, which is the opposite of a mob. In a mob, people lose themselves. In an assembly, people act together but remain individually responsible for behavior. Moreover, on the cross, Jesus became the ultimate scapegoat. By *identifying* with the scapegoat, He revealed that there is no such person as an "outsider." There is no such person as an "enemy." *Everyone* is a member of the human family and, therefore, is our brother and sister. We cannot exclude anyone from our concern, care, and attention. Of course, we may have to discipline wrong-doers, fight injustice, stand up to dictators, defend ourselves against violence, and urge repentance on many people. But they are all our brothers and sisters in the Garden.

Just-War Theory of St. Augustine

What can a nation justly do when attacked? St. Augustine attempted in the fourth century after Jesus to out-line some basic guidelines to control a response to unjust aggression. Briefly put, a nation may respond with organized warfare directed at the attacker if (1) done in self-defense, (2) the cause is just, (3) the force used is in proportion to the offense, (4) innocent people are spared, and (5) there is a rea-sonable expectation of success. It takes a great deal of honest self-reflection on the part of all citizens in union with legit-imate and responsible leaders to discern their application in any given case. The point of just-war actions is to resist vio-lence to the point where it stops. It is not to take territory, take property, or even punish the perpetrators. It is to stop war as fast as possible.

Some of these conditions are actually hard to find these days. Because of modern communications, it is almost impossible to be surprised by a sneak attack by any military force. There should almost always be ample opportunities for negotiation or political settlements before hostilities begin. Because of the indiscriminate and blanketlike devastation by nuclear, chemical, and biological weapons, there is almost no occasion when these may be used. After all, it would be impossible to discriminate the guilty from the innocent. Because it is relatively easy for any nation or even small group to receive significant lethal weaponry in the international arms trade, it is also difficult even for a large nation to ensure success in war. A rogue state might resort to a nuclear attack when faced with defeat. The conditions for a just war are just very hard to find.

We must remember that the Just-War Theory is still a theory. It is a human attempt guided by Christian tradition to control and regulate the violence of war. It is an attempt to use rational thought to calm the impulse for revenge. We still believe that war is not inevitable or intrinsic to human nature. We believe in the Garden virtues and the message and example of Jesus to unite us as one. "Once I am lifted up, I will draw all people to myself" (John 12:32).

Deterrence

What may a nation do to deter an attack? One idea of deterrence is the threat of Mutual Assured Destruction (MAD). If the reprisal wipes out your nation, you may think again about attacking. The cold war used massive mutual assured destruction successfully to ensure the absence of nuclear war for fifty years. Its main weapon was massive fear. This weapon was seen as better than the alternative, which was nuclear war. Ironically, if an attack were ever made, such massive retaliation would not actually be used, as it would destroy both sides. It was a fiction that worked.

A similar idea in conventional warfare is the threat of massive overriding force. One nation threatens to use so much force that it overwhelms and paralyzes the opponent into submission early in the fight or prevents conflict altogether. If battle begins, massive force attempts to close the fight swiftly before too many people are hurt. It is an adaptation of the idea of using force for the purpose of stopping the fight and not for simply inflicting punishment.

Both ideas involve the collection of massive amounts of very expensive arms. Such a dependence on weaponry can lead to a culture of fear, threat, and anxiety. With guns everywhere, it becomes an easy temptation to use them rather than the more laborious path of negotiations. Therefore, these weapons depend on highly moral, responsible, and legitimate leadership to keep them under control. Their expense is also an economic burden on any country but especially on developing nations. During the cold war, President Eisenhower called money spent on weapons a "theft from the poor."

Deterrence is still a noble goal of political action, but the best deterrent of war remains trust. After all, no Americans feared the massive nuclear arsenal of Great Britain or France during the cold war. We trusted them, and it worked. Weaponry accumulation reveals a breakdown in trust. The Garden virtues impel us to build trust among nations by honest communication, respect for peoples and the rule of law, and the fair and just use of the world's resources.

Terrorism

An official state of war is rarely declared anymore, and nations rarely initiate violence against other nations. Violence on a global scale most often comes from smaller groups within nations, such as rebel forces, paramilitary units, and terrorists.

International terrorism is a new form of old warfare. It is the preferred form of violence by small political groups that cannot afford huge armies or the expense of complex weaponry. It makes special use of violence and fear. A terrorist group tries to frighten many people into compliance by the violent actions of a few. It uses the power of sudden and horrific atrocities to injure or kill a few people in order to frighten many into submission. It has the same effect as a lever on which a small movement can lift a great weight with little effort.

Nations tend to look upon these groups as armed and dangerous criminal organizations that have broken the law with deadly force, much as we would view the Ku Klux Klan and other white supremacist groups. Their terrorist actions are crimes, and so nations feel justified in using deadly force against these "criminals." However, the victim nation must respond lawfully and justly. The response must be the same as any police action: Find and bring to justice the perpetrators. Terrorism as a response to terrorism is wrong.

Business Morality: Can a Moral Business Be Financially Successful?

In your family, you already know who the honest people are. However, in a global economy we often deal with people whom we do not know at all. How can we know who will keep their word? If business is about buying and selling, how can we be sure we are dealing with trustworthy people? Fortunately, moral rules developed to guide the transactions of strangers so that they would act like trusted family members.

Business today is full of legal and ethical rules: some mandated by force, some by voluntary agreements. Business usually works well to the extent that people keep these rules. In fact, government agencies monitor businesses closely to make sure that happens. But what about behavior that is not governed by law? Is everything that is legal also moral? More importantly, can a business be both moral and financially successful?

> *We believe that the same behaviors that ensure*
> *a happy moral life will likely promote*
> *a successful business life.*

After all, a business is about *relationships* with key groups of people such as owners, customers, and employees, as well as vendors, competitors, regulators, and even neighborhood communities. These are people, not products or things, and ensuring their well being and satisfaction usually translates into business success. We believe that the basic ideas that make any personal relationship successful can apply to these business relationships as well. After all, people do not buy or sell based on price alone. The person buying or selling is a human filled with hopes, dreams, expectations, and impressions about what this particular transaction will do for him or her. For example, this car will provide happiness, success, love, sex, or meaning. Buying and selling must address the whole person to be successful. That is also moral. We believe every human being is made in the image of God, and so those companies that respect the virtues of *goodness, equality, freedom,* and *service* to self and others that were revealed to Adam and Eve in the Garden of Eden ensure good business ethics and likely financial success.

Business can do wonderful things. It can provide meaningful work and a sense of accomplishment to both owners and employees. It can increase the wealth and influence of nations. It can provide needed goods and services to customers. However, what a company sells and how it advertises are ethically important but often difficult to assess morally. Is this or that product moral just because people want it? What about marketing violent games for children? How do we decide what is a "moral" product? We can picture different products lying somewhere on a continuous scale with *moral* at one end and *immoral* on the other. The degree to which anything causes harm or offends against the Garden virtues moves it closer to the bad end. Of course, people are certainly capable of buying things that are against their own best interests, even if legal, such as excessive alcohol or tobacco. Harmful products may be legal and still be immoral in that they lower our goodness and dignity as persons. While some endanger our health, like tobacco, others appeal to more primitive instincts of violence, like certain video games.

Business helps people get what they want, for which they are willing to pay a fair price. But what is a "fair" price? A fair price comes naturally from the balance of supply, demand, and whatever people are willing to pay. For example, in a free market, prices find their natural level. A free market prevents either buyer or seller from arbitrarily setting prices too high or low. However, if a man wants to pay millions for a painting, well, we can be sure the seller will let him! That painting now "equals" (in dollars, not aesthetics) the price paid. That exchange should be seen *clearly* to be open and fair and not secretly manipulated. That is why insider trading, monopolies, and price-fixing are so wrong. Fairness means that everyone can see the whole playing field clearly and that the two items exchanged are equal in value. Equality of exchange protects the dignity of all parties. Customers get what they want for a fair price, owners get a fair return on their investment, and employees get a fair compensation. Everyone "profits." Everyone's interests are balanced against those of the others. That openness and fairness form some of the foundations of business morality.

Sometimes a company can create desire or demand for a product when there was none before, with effective marketing and advertising. Nothing is wrong with that as long as the marketing is truthful, clear, and fair, especially to those with limited judgment, such as children. After all, the company (made up of people) is dealing with customers (who are people, too). Each one is created by God with a dignity that is deserving of respect. The truthful company respects the right of customers to have enough valid product knowledge to make informed choices on a purchase. Of course, consumers also know that such words as, "the best!" "new and improved!" and "amazing results!" are hyperbole. They are taken with the same credence we have for a person who responds to "How are you?" with, "Fine!" even if that is not the case. These common advertising words are not taken at face value, and so there is no high *expectation* of truth. However, a deliberate and substantially false or misleading product claim, when there is an expectation of truth, seriously hinders the right of consumers to know the value of the exchange.

While the overuse of certain words degrades their power to communicate, the exaggerated use of sexual and violent imagery degrades respect for persons. It encourages the use of persons as objects for personal pleasure or gain. Nothing could be further from the purpose for which we were created! The cumulative effect over time of ads, media, or products that debase persons, religions, relationships, families, or other important values can create a climate of disrespect. Because consumers become habituated to these images quickly, companies may even escalate their intensity and graphical power, making the situation worse. The bar for bad taste gets lower and lower. Although it is difficult to avoid offensive billboards and TV commercials, both consumers and companies share, to some degree, responsibility for not producing or tolerating ads or products that offend our dignity as human persons.

In every commercial transaction, the business mainly enters into relationships with three key groups: owners, customers, and employees. These relationships reveal the source of moral ideas in business, even in today's fiercely competitive global economy. We believe the basic rules that make any relationship work apply to these business relationships as well. Many ethical and legal rules exist to ensure that these relationships are *free and voluntary*. Neither customers, owners, nor employees have to stay with a company. Therefore, successful companies must treat all their key groups well in order to maintain the relationship. That means they must provide at least basic needs for human interaction, such as respect, freedom, and opportunities to grow and prosper. The following is a brief and general application of some of the Garden virtues to business.

Freedom, Equality, Goodness, and Service Applied to Business Ethics

1. *Respecting equality by honesty in communications:*

   a. Ensuring truth and clarity in advertising, memos, reporting, policies.

   b. Providing full and fair product disclosure; no "bait and switch" tactics.

   c. Keeping owners, customers, and employees appropriately informed.

2. *Respecting freedom to choose and fairness of trading:*

a. Setting fair pricing, ensuring free and open markets; no monopolies.

b. Respecting limited judgment of children in the market-place.

c. Offering timely service; no insider trading; no bribery.

d. Giving honest pay for honest work; giving everyone what is their due.

3. *Respecting the goodness and dignity of persons:*

a. Making legal, safe, and morally appropriate products.

b. Ensuring both freedom from harassment and access to all labor laws and rights.

c. Providing polite and professional service to customers.

d. Providing proper training and resources for employees.

e. Respecting company physical and intellectual property.

4. *Respecting our being helpmates:*

a. Using no shortcuts on operation or product standards.

b. Ensuring a safe work environment and proper maintenance of equipment.

c. Providing proper training and resources for employees.

d. Being a good neighbor in the community; philan-thropic support.

e. Being environmentally responsible.

Many of these ideas ensure a "level playing field" so that competition between companies is open and fair and free. They ensure that the consumer has enough information to make an informed choice about a product. They ensure respect for each person. They ensure the right conditions for competition, profit making, lobbying, and success.

Competition, Profits, Taxes, and Success

Competition today is fierce. Some recent advice books on business use combat or warfare metaphors to describe the climate of competition today. They imagine the marketplace as a *jungle, a war, a dog-eat-dog place* or business people as *warriors*. They foster a spirit that says, "Nice guys finish last." Some say that making excessive profit is the only goal and that any tactic is useful to make the "almighty dollar." Sometimes a short-term use of dishonest or aggressive tactics can help land an immediate sale. However, that can actually make matters worse for a company. Because every commercial transaction is between persons or involves corporations that act as persons, the same actions that harm relationships can actually harm business success in the long run. Customers, and even employees, will eventually discover a company's deceit and wonder if they will be the next victims. Customers and employees may not trust a company that acts in such total self-interest and may move on to another company. There is nothing better for a company than a *happy and loyal* customer (or employee) who returns again and again for business with a trusted company.

The essence of that business relationship is trust. Ultimately, a customer or employee trusts that the company is worth the exchange of his or her money or employment.

Ironically, too much competition is bad for business. The more successful companies look for those market niches in which there is a great demand and little or no competition. They want to be "the first with the most" in a new market. They also focus more on improving their own product as opposed to trying only to destabilize others. For example, people will pay a lot of money for certain cars because the cars are made well and are unique, even though they could easily buy much cheaper cars at a nearby store.

Profits, of course, keep a company going. Profit is a good thing. There are many Gospel stories in which Jesus supports the goodness of making a profit (e.g., Matt 25:14; Luke 19:12). *Fair* profit is even better because it means you will probably have return customers. Anything that hinders fairness, such as a monopoly that uses price gouging or price fixing, causes resentment among customers. They will leave at the first chance. If the company ever loses its monopoly position, it will lose its angry customers too. People do not like being forced into relationships, and that is what monopolies do. For example, our excessive reliance on expensive oil from the OPEC cartel in the 1970s caused resentment and motivated the United States to build large oil reserves as well as to explore our own new sources of oil. We worked hard to *free ourselves from the necessity* of buying foreign oil.

Taxes, especially avoiding taxes, is a prime area of moral discussion. Taxes redistribute wealth to provide for the common good of communities, such as for police and fire services, as well as fund the very agencies that keep businesses fair and honest. Our taxes also provide for important aid and help to the poor. However, they are compulsory and so do not involve our personal decision to help others. Therefore, we are not obligated to be generous to the government that compels our payment. We can avoid paying as much as legally allowed. Although we may morally seek to pay the least possible legal amount in taxes, our personal obligation to be a helpmate and to provide care for others in need remains. In the same manner, corporations are also legal "persons" and so also have a moral obligation to help their community outside of what is compelled by taxation.

Sometimes companies, unions, or corporations seek to influence social or political events that affect their business by supporting causes in the community not directly related to the business. Companies lobby for certain issues to present a desired image to customers, to improve their prospects for profits, or even for genuine, altruistic reasons. These "altruistic" actions can produce good will that translates into increased sales. They are certainly in the company's self-interest—but in the same way that acts of kindness from husband to wife enhance their marriage. We would not call a husband selfish for acting in a way that keeps his wife happy and perhaps inspires her to love him a little more in return. However, when a company decides to act, it represents both owners and employees, so they must participate in those decisions in a fair manner. Sometimes a company will support a cause that an employee opposes. The employee must decide how seriously continued employment compromises his or her integrity and whether or not to stay.

Success is what everyone wants in business and in life. Although there are many definitions of success, they do not always agree. One view is that success is the *feeling of self-esteem* when we have done well. This feeling comes from a combination of praise and accomplishment. Praise without accomplishment is just flattery, whereas accomplishment without praise may lead to resentment. Together, they help us feel successful. We believe the more noble the accomplishment, the greater the potential for a feeling of success. We believe God designed us to feel especially good about achieving goals that are noble and good. It helps to understand the larger picture of the whole work process as well as our part in it. For example, when asked about his job, a commercial aircraft assembly worker might reply, "I help reunite families at Thanksgiving!" He sees the more noble meaning of his labor. However, a worker at an illegal drug manufacturing plant cannot reply, "I simply mix chemicals." We are accountable for every step as well as the end result of what our work accomplishes.

A feeling of real moral success at business comes from achieving the right goals, not just any goals. You may succeed at making money but will not achieve the *fullest feeling of success* God intended for you to have if you did so by lying or cheating your way to the top or by producing something harmful to others. We believe God designed us to feel especially fulfilled, successful, and meaningful by working toward (and accomplishing if possible) very noble goals. Just making money is not noble enough. Money alone is not the measure

of success because it cannot by itself bring the deep fulfillment God plans for us. In fact, in the scriptures, the *love* of
money (not money itself) is the root of evil (1 Tim 6:10; Heb
13:5). However, money is a very useful tool for the one who
knows how to use it for good. Accomplishing that good end
can bring a great feeling of success to everyone in the business. A moral company can be quite successful if the right
decisions are made.

Moral Decision Making in Business

There is a later chapter in this book that describes
moral decision making for individuals. However, it is different in business in which decisions involve choices a company or corporation makes *on behalf* of others, many of
whom may not know that the decision is even being made
for them. A decision might also be on behalf of persons who
may not be Christian, religious, or even ethical. Here are
some generic questions to ask for business decision making
in those tough areas in which it is difficult to decide and in
which the setting is not open to specifically religious guidance. Moreover, business decisions often must be made
quickly, without all the information one would like to have.
Here are some questions that can help keep the company on
a moral path to success even under the pressure of a soon
approaching decision deadline.

Questions to Ask for Moral Decision Making

1. Does a decision actually *have* to be made now?

2. Do I have as much information as I can have *right now?*

3. Is the decision legal?

4. Will this decision compromise *public health or safety?*

5. Is our decision in line with our *corporate philosophy or mission?*

6. How will it effect our *owners, customers, employees, and neighborhood?*

7. What if the decision were *publicly known?*

8. What if this decision were done to *my family or me?*

Our answers to these questions will directly affect important relations with owners, customers, and employees and, above all, yourself. You may find that you disagree with the direction the company is taking or the moral decisions made. You must decide what to do: continue to work for change from within the company; seek redress from outside authorities, such as government agencies; or simply leave. You can view it as you would decisions about maintaining or changing relationships in your personal life, such as with (a) a spouse, (b) a friend, or (c) an acquaintance. Each of these relationships makes different demands of your commitment.

You will have different levels of interest in maintaining each relationship if it becomes problematic. For example, you might work hard to improve the relationship with your spouse when you both disagree but let that with the acquaintance go. You are just not as committed to the acquaintance or as willing to work for change as with a spouse. Your moral path will depend on the level of relationship you have with the company and the level of offense that is being directed at you as a person worthy of respect and dignity. Some situations we tolerate, others we should not. We must always remember that we cannot allow ourselves to be seriously mistreated. We must make some response.

One of the most famous cases of business ethics involved the Tylenol poisoning event of a few years ago. When someone poisoned a few bottles of Tylenol, a popular headache and pain medication, several customers died. Johnson & Johnson, the makers of Tylenol, quickly applied similar guidelines to make a decision. They consulted their corporate culture, which places a major emphasis on maintaining and fostering their key relationships, and applied it to this case. They considered their relationships as a major company commitment. The owners knew they were *also* victims of a crime and had done nothing wrong. Even so, they immediately pulled more than $250 million worth of inventory off the shelves and repackaged new products with tamperproof lids. They did so not knowing the future economic effects on the company but knowing that they would not compromise on the well being of the *people with whom they are in a committed business relationship*. It resulted in a massive surge of customer trust and loyalty and a subsequent hefty increase in profits. It is possible to be moral as well as financially successful when the right decisions are made.

Professional Morality: Medicine, Law, and Psychotherapy

Some areas of life, such as medicine, the law, and mental health, are just too complicated to handle on our own. Very few people can do their own surgery, defend themselves in court, or treat their own depression by themselves. People can suffer much without proper assistance. Medical, legal, or mental problems require expert care, so we place them in the hands of specialists who have the training and education to assess, diagnose, and treat those issues. While specialists seem to work in such widely different fields, they all provide important help *as a professional service for money*. While medicine, law, and therapy are the most familiar professions and have their unique standards of professional conduct, the general ethical and moral guidelines are similar across many fields.

The professional is doing work for a client, who pays a fair price for the service. The client is paying for the training and education the client does not have or for work the client cannot do for him- or herself. The professional is acting only the client's behalf and in his or her best interests, almost as a kind of "trustee." The professional is acting and making informed decisions as if he or she were the client, only with more specialized education. It is a relationship of trust. As we saw in the section on business ethics, all the behaviors that enhance trust, such as knowledge, honesty, and integrity, contribute to an ethical professional relationship.

The professional is in business and so provides the service for a price. That is the principal exchange: fee for service. The professional must only provide help that is truly in the best interests of the client and is consistent with the generally accepted practice and must only receive money or its equivalent in return. At a minimum, the professional must "do no harm." Of course, we hope the professional might receive a great sense of fulfillment in helping other people, but he or she cannot use the client for any other personal gain. Once the client enters into a professional business relationship, his or her treatment needs come first.

Because of the very high cost of some of these services, some professions have organized to provide help in a "rationed," way, such as HMOs in medicine or legal clinics in the law. Although this helps in some ways to make service more affordable, especially for low-income clients, there is a danger that certain benefits, such as high-cost medical testing or a client's preferred physician, will not be provided. While many places make sure that both the law and medicine provide basic services for free, such as a Public Defender's Office in the law or ambulance services from the Fire Department, professions are not required to provide more specialized assistance without pay. The client needs to have full disclosure about his or her options about available services and their costs to make an informed choice about how to proceed.

Medical, legal, and mental problems can make us weak and vulnerable. Faced with a sudden crisis, such as an arrest or disease, some people find it hard to think straight and make wise choices. The professional can provide that much needed expert advice and help, in the greatest tradition of our nature as helpmates. That means the professional treats the client as a person, worthy of full human dignity and respect, not as an opportunity for exploitation at a difficult time. That means the professional starts, continues, *and also stops* service when appropriate. The professional works to restore the client to a position of strength and competence, whether medical, legal, or mental.

Clients are always in charge of their treatment program. After all, it is their life and they are ultimately responsible for it. They must decide what is best for themselves. That means clients must receive as timely, accurate, and complete information as they need concerning their diagnosis and treatment options. The professional becomes both their healer and their wise teacher.

Sometimes we use the word *counselor* to describe the role professionals play in our lives. That is a wonderful word. A counselor provides wise advice to a person in need, whether for an arrest, a disease, or a lack of life training. Wise counselors can help with prevention as well as recovery. That means we receive advice on how not to get into trouble in the first place. For example, a doctor can advise us to quit smoking, even though there are no detrimental symptoms yet. A lawyer can advise us to change a business practice even though it may or may not be legal to take someone to court.

A therapist, of course, can help with behaviors that will more likely keep our relationships intact. Wise counselors help prevent problems from ever happening.

A moral professional acts in the very best tradition of the Garden virtues. For a fair price, they help those in need and at all times respect the equality, goodness, and freedom of their clients.

Discussion Starters

1. What do you think society should do with people who abuse children?

2. What are your thoughts about legalizing drugs?

3. Describe your feelings about morality in the business world.

4. Do you have any moral concerns about your present job or company?

5. Describe a time when someone seriously hurt you. What were your feelings toward that person? Did they change over time?

6. What are your thoughts about the phrase, "love your enemies"? Why do you think Jesus would say this?

CHAPTER 5

Deciding What to Do

There comes a moment when we must finally decide what to do. As always, our goal is to choose behavior that fulfills our God-given nature to love. But is there a good process we can use to help us do this? What process is the most honest? Certainly we can use the list of questions found in the section on business morality as a start. You may already have developed something similar for yourself. It is important to have some system on which you can depend. The moment of decision is dramatic, for the consequences may be long-lasting and effect your life and possibly the lives of others for some time. It is also helpful to recognize the stages of decision making.

You might have already found this pattern to be the way you have made moral choices in your life so far. One model has five stages: There is (a) the "John the Baptist" stage when you first get the idea to do something, just as John the Baptist first inspired people to follow Jesus; (b) the wavering and investigative stage in which you wonder what to do; (c) the "John Wayne" stage of courage in which you finally decide; (d) another wavering stage in which you have doubts about the choice; and (e) the peace stage in which you receive some form of confirmation about your choice. Some confusion is natural in all this, but our goal is to end up feeling confident in our decision. Having a plan greatly helps in stressful times.

Important decisions often involve intense feelings and emotions. That makes it even more difficult to decide clearly. Having a road map helps. If indecision becomes a habit, then it helps even more! Here are some steps in making moral decisions honestly. They are really commonsense ideas for deciding with integrity and ensuring a sense of peace with the result.

Gather Facts

1. Know as much as you can about the issue; take the time to study it well.

2. Distinguish between what you know for certain and what is uncertain.

3. List the possible choices, and keep revising as you learn more.

4. List all the people who are or will be affected by each choice and why.

5. Determine as best you can the consequences of each choice.

Gather Resources

1. Assemble and prioritize as many scripture passages, opinions, and teachings as you can. Don't avoid or fear any source, but use the following sources first.

a. *Scripture*

   1. Seek direct and indirect references about the issue.

   2. Try to discover the spirit of the passage and the intent of the author.

b. *Church Teachings*

   1. Seek how Catholics have believed and taught this topic through the ages.

   2. Assess how forceful or consistent the teaching has been over time.

c. *Theological and Secular Opinion*

   1. How are the different opinions consistently supported by wise experts?

   2. Gather the ideas, feelings, and opinions of wise family members, friends, and people that you respect.

d. *Legal and Ethical Laws and Guidelines*

   1. Determine the legal issues and/or professional, ethical standards of the case as they apply.

2. If the final choices are conflicting, determine which resources are more authoritative from revelation, are more important to the Garden virtues, and have more lasting consequences.

Prayer

1. Seek wisdom from God and His will for you.

2. Ask that your choice be the one Jesus Himself would make.

3. Ask for courage and honesty.

Decide

1. Make your choice in the very human loneliness of a personal decision, recognizing that you are often choosing between two or more good behaviors.

2. Choose with God as your witness and what you believe God calls you to do.

3. Choose *as if* your decisions always would be made public.

4. Choose the option you would be willing to have happen to you or your family.

Accept Consequences

1. This is one of the definitions of maturity and responsibility because your decision may bring results that are difficult or that place you in dissent.

   a. Consequences may be a natural result of your choice.

b. Remember that God wants you to be honest with yourself.

Be Humble

1. Be open to change, reevaluation, and reappraisal.

Church Leaders and Moral Teachings

Bishops cannot create revelation. They are spokespersons of what has always been believed from the beginning, for there is no new revelation or message from God necessary for salvation. All that we need for salvation has been revealed through Jesus in the scriptures and tradition. But not all that Jesus taught was written down. Oral tradition preserved the rest, and it was passed on year after year. Jesus did not speak about everything under the sun either. From the very beginning, the apostles had to derive additional important moral guides from their sense of the Lord's teachings on related issues and their own prayer (1 Cor 7:25). The most important issues of all are declared infallible because they are so fundamental to faith. Jesus guarantees in those crucial areas that there are no mistakes. "I will be with you always" (Matt 28:20).

There is an order of priorities to the other teachings. Some are more important than others. *How consistent, how often, and with what force a teaching is presented determines its importance among Catholics.* There is an order to teaching sources also. Because of the role Jesus granted to the church community assembled under its leaders, the teachings of bishops are given more weight than those of individual theologians or of secular opinion. As always, all opinions are encouraged in the quest to discover the will of God in our life, but there is a difference between an opinion and a teaching. Only the church, under its leaders can give a formal teaching. We believe that is the way Jesus designed His message to stay safe and sound from our individual propensity to choose so often against our own best interests. That is why we try to give that kind of teaching a sincere hearing in our hearts and, if we still have doubts, to pray for the openness to understand and assent. In the end, it matters not so much what I would like or not like, *but what is the mind of Jesus Christ*. It is He who we follow. It is His name that we call ourselves. We are Christians.

Your Conscience and Dissent

A Catholic can "in good conscience" follow that personal conscience, even if it is in dissent from noninfallible church teaching, if all the conscience-forming steps have been followed sincerely and honestly. We cannot base dissent on a "whim" or feeling of the moment and certainly not on a passing fad. Because God created us as rational beings, we should have reasons for what we do. We want to be honest about these things, so we should take the time to inform our conscience and follow it. That is simply being authentic. Ultimately we all stand before the Lord alone, completely responsible for our own thoughts and behavior. We should stand before him responsibly and authentically. That means we have to do some homework.

Even so, there are some behaviors that are always wrong in all cases. These are the ones that infringe on the Garden virtues and are clearly written in the Ten Commandments. Most of these commandments are negatives, or "shalt nots." They represent the lower limits of behavior below which we cannot go. The rest are positives, such as honoring parents, and offer upper goals for behavior. They are more generic and not as clear as the negatives, though. For example, "honoring parents" is not as clear as "don't kill." But negatives are useful for that clarity and lower-limit setting. While we may not be able to love people very much, at least we don't kill them! That is an absolute lower limit to behavior. In no way can we ever treat another person as a thing to be used, as a mere object.

However, if in all humility and honesty a person still feels, believes, and thoughtfully understands that his or her choice of a dissenting opinion is the one God calls him or her to live, it must be followed. We must still call the action itself wrong even though personal culpability and responsibility before God might be lessened by an informed and sincere decision of conscience. Subjectively, the person is moral before the Lord. Objectively, he or she may differ from both the Lord's will and His community and as such may or may not be able to enjoy community life fully, for example, receiving communion, which after all is a public and visible sign of the unity of belief. Subjective sincerity does not mean there are no objective consequences. After all, I may firmly disagree with certain governmental policies, but I must still pay taxes.

However, if a person cannot accept even the most basic beliefs about Catholicism, then it makes sense to accept the most honest name for him- or herself: non-Catholic. This is probably the hardest area in all of morality to accept because it sounds so exclusionary. Yet, it is that powerful precisely because it challenges such long-standing habits of thinking. It simply affirms the truth of things and the reality of a person's personal religious outlook. Of course, the church would like everyone to follow its way, but it also safeguards the God-given freedom we have to follow our informed conscience. Of course, God would like us to follow Him, but He allows us complete freedom while we live here on Earth to go our own way. We must simply call ourselves by the authentic name of who we are and how we live. It is not easy to follow Jesus; yet His more difficult teachings challenge us to see and think more deeply. The rewards, as people have found for more than twenty centuries, are profoundly satisfying.

Some still turn away, however, and travel on a path away from Jesus. That has certainly happened a few times in history! What can our attitude be toward them? As we saw earlier in the Gospel, Jesus meets a rich young man, who asks, "What must I do to achieve eternal life?" (Mark 10:17 and Matt 19:16). Certainly, that is the ultimate question. Jesus lays out a very complete and crystal clear two-part answer, but the man refuses to accept it and walks away. Interestingly, Jesus lets him go, for He will not interfere with the man's free will; yet He still looks at him with love. Despite the rejection, Jesus still loves the rich, young man. But Our Lord will not change His story to get the man back.

The road to a moral life remains the same no matter what our response. All kinds of people have rejected this road, from Adam and Eve, to the man in the Gospel, down to many examples today. Yet the Christian response remains the same, as it must. *We believe there is a way to eternal life; it has been revealed and lived by Jesus; and we mean to follow it.* If others do not, we are sad. We wish their response was different, but we look at them with love, and we deeply respect their freedom. We can do no more or less than the Lord Himself.

Confession

Because it is often difficult to make good choices, we will occasionally make mistakes, sometimes in serious matters. A whole series of questions can spring to mind. How do we get back on track? Can we really start over? What are the lingering effects of these mistakes? Does God ever hold a grudge? How do we make peace with our past failures? What should be our attitude toward our own sinfulness? What are mortal and venial sins? How does confession operate? These are important questions because of the very powerful effect that misplaced guilt plays in the lives of many people. Because some misguided teachers in the past declared even little mistakes to be serious mortal sins, many people today are reluctant to admit *any sins at all*. Their fear of misplaced shame motivates them to rationalize or even minimize their sins. Others, however, may live in total fear of a God who seems ready to pounce on their every human foible. They maximize every weakness into a mortal sin worthy of eternal damnation.

Confession is meant to be a free and easy place in which we can be honest with God and ourselves about our life. *God is more interested in how fast we can recover and get back on the right moral track.* It is repentance, recovery, and change that He desires, not retribution, punishment, or revenge. In almost every biblical reference to sin, Jesus emphasizes more the act of repentance and change. God is not surprised, shocked, or dismayed by our sins. After all, they are somewhat expected, thanks to Adam and Eve. He is only interested in our rapid recovery so that we can quickly have the joy that comes from living His way. While it is possible to be sinless with His grace, it doesn't happen to often. God does not expect perfection as much as He does honesty.

That we sin says little about our character except that we are human. That we repent, recover, and change says everything about our character, and indicates that we are real Christians. While Judas betrayed Jesus, he also despaired of reconciliation. Peter betrayed Jesus three times! However, he returned to be reconciled, learned from his mistakes and changed. Despite his far worse sin, Peter was made the first pope because he was honest with himself and the Lord about his sin and he learned and changed from it. That is precisely the kind of person Jesus called to lead the first Christians!

These ideas about confession and God's grace can change our fear into courage. We need not fear to look at ourselves honestly and to admit mistakes. Why should we? God has made it easy to be honest, and that honesty can help us live in the truth, which is much better than any fantasy world of pseudoperfection. That world is too hard to maintain.

If fear of confession in the past or excessive guilt or a remembered voice of harsh judgment has prevented us from acknowledging *any* sins, well, let us fear no longer. The real story of confession is liberation, the freedom we feel to be real, genuine, and authentic before the Lord. We can easily and without embarrassment present our mistakes to God.

Making a thoughtful examination of conscience is crucial to this experience. It means we have reflected seriously and conscientiously. It means we *want* to know ourselves better—the good and the bad. Remember that self-knowledge gives us a sense of balance and perspective and that this is the beginning of wisdom. Reflecting on the past few days or weeks helps us see the patterns of our life and the general direction of our behavior. Are we happy with the path? What does our behavior reveal about our values?

The penance given is a good thing for us as well. It is not a punishment for sins by which we earn our forgiveness. God's forgiveness is freely given. Penance is simply a real and practical recommended action or prayer for spiritual renewal. It points to the future and a new way of living honestly with God. It says we have changed for the better. The priest simply recommends some prayer or action that will reinforce the new lessons of virtue learned from our self-examination and the experience of God's forgiveness.

Confession should be that kind of renewal experience for us. Confession can be a place where we easily, honestly, and sincerely acknowledge ourselves as we are before the Lord. It is an act of truth, not submission. After all, during the penitential rite at Mass we stand at our full height in a wonderful sign of personal dignity when we confess our sinfulness. Our act of honesty reveals the very best in human behavior, the authentic truth about ourselves, and our need for the Lord. There is nothing more natural than that.

Discussion Starters

1. Describe the people in your life whom you would consider wise and with whom you would consult if faced with an important moral issue.

2. What is your reaction when the church teaches a moral position with which you strongly agree? Strongly disagree?

3. With which areas of church moral teaching are you most in dissent? In agreement? Describe briefly why you hold these views.

4. How do you feel just before you are going to confession? How do you feel just after?

5. What do you feel are the five most important beliefs someone must hold in order to be called Christian?

CHAPTER 6

Final Thoughts

Religion is not something "extra" in a person. We cannot see it merely as an option or just something for those so inclined. It is our *nature* to be religious and to have a sense of how to relate to God (with praise) and with each other (with love). These moral or behavioral guides are not imposed arbitrarily on us by some outside source. They are not the result of some large, unfeeling, or foreign bureaucracy. They're not from "outside" ourselves at all. They arise from deep inside, where God put them when He created us (Heb 8:10). Religion as an institution simply makes public what is in our God-given nature, and God created us with a deep sense of faith. He created us to love. Then His joy will be ours, and our joy will be complete!

Catholic moral behavior is always an attempt to return to the Garden of Eden. From Abraham, throughout the Old Testament, and especially through the life of Jesus, and now through His people the church, God has invited us to return to our true human nature, which He designed to balance love of God, others, and self. We occasionally change that nature and get our life out of balance with too much or too little love in one or more areas. "Getting" easily overtakes "giving" in our life. *Catholics believe there is a way to live that is better than others, and it is the way to live made by God and lived by His Son, Jesus Christ.* Anyone, of any faith, can live that life and find true fulfillment and salvation. We believe strongly that God meant for us to be happy, satisfied, and fulfilled, even in a difficult world. "I have come that you might have life and joy, and have it to the fullest and most complete!" (John 10:10; 15:11).

The themes of this book have focused on knowing and living the moral life. The beginning sections revealed the relationship between Adam and Eve before the fall as the norm of all moral behavior. They were created in the image of God to be *free, equal, good, and helpmates* to each other in loving service. All of our own behavior is moral if it enhances, protects, and encourages those very same virtues.

Behavior is immoral if it deters, interferes, or prevents these virtues from their fulfillment. All moral guidelines simply let us be the people God made us to be. They enable us to live the equality, goodness, freedom, and service we were designed to live. They also preserve the dignity and value we have as the people for whom God was even willing to send His Son (John 3:16).

When those virtues were applied to various issues, such as premarital sex, our understanding revealed that sexual activity is another form of talking, using the language of the body instead of words. That has a larger point in moral thinking. All our behavior speaks. Our behavior must speak equality, mutuality, freedom, and service to each other. In fact, the message of *all behavior* must communicate these Garden of Eden virtues.

159

This book focused on why we believe what we do about moral behavior. However, we cannot live it perfectly all the time. Mistakes are guaranteed in our life because of Original Sin. Yet this most common occurrence can cause so much damage because of misplaced guilt and misunderstandings. We need to understand conscience formation, guilt, and dissent. Conscience is the voice that tells us to do or not do something. Guilt is the voice we hear after the act and tells us whether it was right or not. Our intellect helps us determine what choices are available and what the good things to do are. However, only God can determine what is truly good. *We must discern what He has already determined is the truth.* We believe that there is a way that is better than all the others and that it has been revealed and lived by Jesus, and we aim to follow it. He is more than a model of good living. After all, so were Socrates, Aristotle, and Confucius. We believe Jesus was the Son of God and the ultimate way, truth, and life. Fortunately, Jesus, *as the Son of God,* actually provides the grace to follow Him on this path. Faith in the Lord opens rivers of courage, strength, and grace. Let us never fear to call on Him to help us in our great moral decisions.

Dissent clarified the relationship between our view and the natural law views of reality. Dissent is a real possibility in moral matters, and it is important to know what are the degrees to which one can differ from church teachings and still be Catholic. Infallible and noninfallible teachings and the hierarchy of teachings, or the priority of truths, help us put things in perspective. For noninfallible ideas, we look to the *intensity* of the church's teaching, its *duration* in history, and the *frequency* of repetition of certain teachings for indications of how strongly they are held and how close they are to the core of Christian beliefs. We cannot reject infallible teachings and remain Catholic.

This is a very important idea because these concepts are so very often misused and misunderstood. People want to have clear guidelines given in a nonjudgmental way about where they stand and how to make that determination about themselves. After all is said and done, we need to be able to see where our ideas and behaviors fit into or out of the Catholic world. Above all, we need to see the difference between holding ideas on some kind of a whim and the serious and honest investigation of what God has said about various issues. It is not enough to just go with our first impressions or feelings about an issue. We must seek the will of God through much prayer, study, discussion, and humility. Simply put, Jesus is either true or not true. If true, He is worth taking seriously.

Finally again, we believe that Catholic moral understanding is rooted in our human nature. No religious bureaucracy could ever impose such a widespread practice with such a pervasive record in human history as morality. Religion is not something imposed or forced on us by some outside institution. It could never have been that successful over such a long time in human history. People eventually rise up and against unjust guilt or power or force. Religion is not so much imposed as discovered. It is discovered within—already present in our hearts—waiting to be acknowledged and expressed. It is discovered from under layers of forgetfulness at times and when finally expressed can be extraordinarily fulfilling. It is as natural as the feeling of love.

When we feel that awesome presence of God, we just naturally want to do something about it. What we do is live a life that is good, free, respectful, and helpful to others. We live a moral life and at last find the peace and joy promised us from the very beginning of the world.

Resources

A. Web Sites

Catholics on the Internet (1997), Brother John Raymond, Prima Publishing, Rocklin, Calif.

The Internet is a rich source of church documentation today. Search engines also can easily find Web sites about specific moral issues. This book, edited by Brother Raymond, contains hundreds of Internet sites on religious topics. Here are a few sites that are especially helpful.

http://listserv.american.edu/catholic/church/church.html/
This site contains many informative and relevant church documents concerning moral topics.

http://www.catholic.com
This is the Web site for Catholic Answers. This site specializes in explaining complex issues clearly and concisely. Both sites have links to other sites as well.

B. Books

Brown, Raymond E., Joseph A. Fitzmyer, and Roland E. Murphy, editors. *The New Jerome Biblical Commentary.* Englewood Cliffs, N.J.: Prentice Hall, 1990.

This is the most complete biblical commentary available. Any books by Raymond Brown are usually very concise, clear, and compelling reading. He is one of the world's foremost biblical scholars and a member of the Pontifical Biblical Commission.

May, William W., *Vatican Authority and the American Catholic Dissent,* New York: Crossroads, 1997.

This is a very thorough and clear explanation of the issues around faith and dissent in a collection of articles from both bishops and theologians.

Our Sunday Visitor Staff. *Catechism of the Catholic Church,* Vatican City: Libreria Editrice Vaticana (English Translation, Second Edition), Huntington, Ind.: Our Sunday Visitor, 2000.

This book is a required resource for anyone who wants an authoritative summary of important Catholic teaching. It provides in one edition a very useful source of official Catholic teaching on a whole range of Catholic subjects.

C. Articles

Bennet, Neil G., Ann Limas Blanc, and David E. Bloom. "Commitment and the Modern Union: Assessing the Link between Premarital Cohabitation and Subsequent Marital Stability," *American Sociological Review.* Vol. 53, 1988, pp. 1227–38

This is one sample article from the research field on cohabitation. These researchers from both Yale and Columbia Universities offer an excellent bibliography of additional studies and reviews for your further research.

■■■ Resources ■■■

Heney, David C. *Cohabitation,* Unpublished manuscript, University of Southern California, Los Angeles, Calif., 1991

This is a thesis for a Master of Science degree in Marriage, Family, and Child Counseling, available from the author. It includes a review of the professional literature from 1970 through 1990. Because no single study can be exhaustive, the pattern developed over many years and across many studies is more valid and reliable.